# Praise for the second edition of *Digital Darwinism*

Big, bold ideas that make you think. SCOTT GALLOWAY, PROFESSOR OF MARKETING, NYU STERN SCHOOL OF BUSINESS, AND BESTSELLING AUTHOR, *THE FOUR* AND *ALGEBRA OF HAPPINESS*

*Digital Darwinism* is a rare call for long-term thinking in a short-term world. Tom Goodwin has a gift for asking questions that don't let you off the hook. With *Digital Darwinism*, he asks some of the most pertinent, well-researched, brilliantly presented and hard to answer questions all businesses brave enough should be asking themselves. SAM CONNIFF, BESTSELLING AUTHOR, *BE MORE PIRATE*, AND DIRECTOR, UNCERTAINTY EXPERTS

*Digital Darwinism* can be a threatening concept, but Tom Goodwin's advice is refreshingly optimistic: don't wait for the perfect moment – embrace change before you have to, change often, focus on possibilities rather than threats and act with common sense and urgency. Whether you're building a start-up or transforming an established legacy brand, you'll find value in Goodwin's perspective. JEFF DAILEY, CEO, FARMERS INSURANCE

The business book leaders need, but don't deserve. ALEX ROY, TV HOST, AND DIRECTOR OF SPECIAL OPERATIONS, ARGO AI

# Praise for the first edition
## of *Digital Darwinism*

A fascinating dip into a disruptive future. DYLAN JONES, FORMER EDITOR, *GQ*, VICE PRESIDENT, HAY FESTIVAL, AND CHAIR, BRITISH FASHION COUNCIL MENSWEAR COMMITTEE

This finally answered many questions about innovation which have long haunted me – not least why most large companies are typically so bad at it. It's one of those rare books that is worth reading twice. RORY SUTHERLAND, VICE CHAIRMAN, OGILVY & MATHER GROUP, AND TED SPEAKER

In a cacophony of voices calling for an immediate digital revolution, how reassuring to hear one advocating a more nuanced and balanced path forwards for your business. How refreshing to have an author parting the weeds of digital transformation, offering homespun, achievable suggestions and solutions for your company. The digital world is littered with a baffling array of jargon and acronyms. Tom Goodwin cuts through the gobbledygook to offer down-to-earth, practical advice for transforming your business. *Digital Darwinism* reassures you that futurizing your company doesn't mean you need to be the next Uber or Amazon of anything. Among the multiple platinum nuggets in this book, the most valuable takeaway is that change must be at the core of your business, not at the edges. Digitally transform your business? First change the way you think about change. ADAM NAJBERG, HEAD OF COMMUNICATIONS, TENCENT GAMES GLOBAL, FORMER HEAD OF DIGITAL MEDIA, ALIBABA, AND DIGITAL EDITOR, *THE WALL STREET JOURNAL ASIA*

In *Digital Darwinism*, Tom Goodwin presents a thoughtful canvas of digital wisdom, covering the past, present and future with smart illustrative examples. It's a great map of the entire digital landscape, sprinkled with invaluable insights to act upon. STEFAN OLANDER, FORMER VICE PRESIDENT, GLOBAL DIGITAL INNOVATION, NIKE

The future does not fit in the containers or mindsets of the past. This book persuades, provokes and points to ways to rethink your business. Society, business and life are being disrupted by a revolutionary stage of evolution: *Digital Darwinism*. This book provides ways to thrive in the new environment. RISHAD TOBACCOWALA, TRANSFORMATION EXPERT, SPEAKER AND WRITER, AND CHIEF GROWTH OFFICER AND MEMBER OF THE MANAGEMENT COMMITTEE, PUBLICIS GROUP

Tom Goodwin delivers what he promises in his preface; the book is wildly irritating at the same time. It is a passionate cry for more common sense in corporate decision making. The examples he provides demonstrate how little companies have embraced the digital age. Goodwin rightly questions the attempts of corporations to overcome disruption and ambiguity in the digital age either by 'better planning' or by minor adjustments to business models and strategies that were developed in a bygone era of stability, linearity and predictability. He reminds us that a flexible response is the only answer to massively changing corporate environments and that entrepreneurship means maximizing opportunities and overcoming obstacles instead of minimizing risks. An overdue book. UWE ELLINGHAUS, FORMER GLOBAL CHIEF MARKETING OFFICER, CADILLAC

*Digital Darwinism* is a must-read for both legacy brands and ambitious start-ups, arming business leaders with clear strategies to navigate disruption, unlock growth and prepare for the future. A bold and provocative thinker, Tom Goodwin brings a fresh approach and a much-needed reminder that you have to think differently in order to win in today's global digital economy. STEFAN LARSSON, CHIEF EXECUTIVE OFFICER, PVH CORP, AND FORMER CEO, RALPH LAUREN

Tom Goodwin sees organizations facing a Darwinian battle for survival, given the pace of technical change. That's familiar ground. What's so refreshing is his notion that empathy will be crucial in that battle – that businesses that put people first are most likely to stay on the right side of the chaos. MARK JONES, FORMER COMMISSIONING EDITOR, *THE WORLD ECONOMIC FORUM AGENDA*, GLOBAL EDITOR, *NETWORKED JOURNALISM*, AND GLOBAL COMMUNITIES EDITOR, *REUTERS NEWS*

Tom Goodwin shows how Darwinian success depends not on ruthlessness but on learning how to play with others. DOUGLAS RUSHKOFF, AUTHOR, *THROWING ROCKS AT THE GOOGLE BUS*

Tom Goodwin is the right kind of futurist: he's a history geek at heart and recognizes that innovation doesn't happen in a vacuum. Context is king, and there's plenty of that in this intelligently constructed book. PAUL KEMP-ROBERTSON, CO-FOUNDER, CONTAGIOUS

If you ever wondered if and how you and your organization could survive and grow in today's disruptive environment, this is the book for you. This beautifully written book offers an informative and insightful description of the age of disruption, the need for a paradigm shift in our thinking and practical guidelines for survival and growth. Enjoy, learn and apply. JERRY WIND, LAUDER PROFESSOR EMERITUS OF MARKETING, THE WHARTON SCHOOL OF THE UNIVERSITY OF PENNSYLVANIA

Today the words 'disruption' and 'innovation' are plastered everywhere. We've become numb to them, lost in a sea of information. The future is here yet it is understood unequally. With *Digital Darwinism*, Tom Goodwin uses his unique combination of passion, empathy and audacity to give us all an equal understanding of the future as it bowls over us. JOHN WINDSOR, THINKER, ADVISER AND ENTREPRENEUR BUILDING PLATFORMS IN THE MARKETING, MEDIA AND INNOVATION INDUSTRIES, AND FOUNDER AND CEO, OPEN ASSEMBLY

# Digital Darwinism

*Surviving the new age*
*of business disruption*

SECOND EDITION

Tom Goodwin

Kogan Page
INSPIRE

First published in Great Britain and the United States in 2018 by Kogan Page Limited
Second edition published 2022

2nd Floor, 45 Gee Street
London
EC1V 3RS
United Kingdom

8 W 38th Street, Suite 902
New York, NY 10018
USA

4737/23 Ansari Road
Daryaganj
New Delhi 110002
India

www.koganpage.com

Kogan Page books are printed on paper from sustainable forests.

**ISBNs**
Hardback      978 1 3986 0194 9
Paperback    978 1 3986 0192 5
Ebook          978 1 3986 0193 2

**British Library Cataloguing-in-Publication Data**
A CIP record for this book is available from the British Library.

**Library of Congress Cataloging-in-Publication Data**
Names: Goodwin, Tom, author.
Title: Digital Darwinism: surviving the new age of business disruption / Tom Goodwin.
Description: Second edition. | New York, NY: Kogan Page, 2022. | Series: Inspire series | Includes bibliographical references and index.
Identifiers: LCCN 2022002955 (print) | LCCN 2022002956 (ebook) | ISBN 9781398601949 (hardback) | ISBN 9781398601925 (paperback) | ISBN 9781398601932 (ebook)
Subjects: LCSH: Electronic commerce. | Technological Innovations–Management.
Classification: LCC HF5548.32 .G666 2022 (print) | LCC HF5548.32 (ebook) | DDC 658/.05–dc23
LC record available at https://lccn.loc.gov/2022002955
LC ebook record available at https://lccn.loc.gov/2022002956

Typeset by Integra Software Services, Pondicherry
Print production managed by Jellyfish
Printed and bound by CPI Group (UK) Ltd, Croydon CR0 4YY

# Contents

# Preface

*The ultimate, hidden truth of the world is that it is something that we make, and could just as easily make differently.* DAVID GRAEBER

This book is about exploring what matters. Throughout history the battle for survival has been driven by a need for more. For more food, more connections, more knowledge. As technology has rewired the planet, we now have more than enough. We first thought of the main battle for communicators as the battle to get someone's time. It's slowly shifted in a world of distractions to be for someone's attention, but in an increasingly chaotic landscape it seems the only thing more valuable than time or attention, is clarity.

One of the curious implications of the mobile phone and algorithmically driven news seems to be our total lack of patience and our inability to extract ourselves from the here and now in front of us (and likely written to stir us) and the broader picture of the world. In many ways the news is rather like a fractal – the more you dig into it, the more there is; the more you refresh your feed, the more news seems to populate it. It's endless, and while its quantity never changes, its significance does. It's rather like the weather: we could measure wind speed and direction or temperature in every square metre of the planet, or for every village or city, or region or country, or as a planet. We could measure it every second, minute, hour, day or month. At some level of granularity, it loses most meaning; at some level of aggregation, it loses resolution. We may seek delight in knowing as much as we can, but at some point it becomes less insightful and more overwhelming. Knowing the price of stock every second is not that useful when it comes to running a company, the trends are. In reality, unless you intend on dynamically pricing ice creams on hot days, most companies really care about long-term climatic patterns more than the hourly weather.

To try to decide what matters is an imposing aim – who am I to know what are absolute truths? Who am I to decide what won't amount to much or to decide what's important to you? Good questions, but I've done my bit to focus on a high-altitude approach, to travel the world to find commonalities, to go to great lengths looking at the past, and to try to focus on a plausible narrative and an enlightening perspective on the changing world. I won't be right, not on everything, but we overvalue correct answers and undervalue statements that make you think, even if they turn out to be wrong.

We are consumed with the idea that we live in an extraordinary time. We consider a global pandemic to be a time of unprecedented unprecedentedness. Millions have died, profound new habits have been set in motion, new business models have thrived, technology has seemingly swept across our world at unprecedented speed, allowing us to do almost anything we want by endlessly tapping away on our personal screens and getting someone less well paid to do it for us. We took school lessons that used to happen in the classroom and totally reimagined the way we could deliver precisely the same lesson on Zoom. Offices around the world were transformed by the shocking notion that you didn't have to spend 74 minutes lugging your body to an office so you could check email at the same time and same places as your colleagues. Now with 5G I can get a slightly faster signal in 10 per cent of my apartment but 100 per cent less signal in the rest of it. Progress is lighting fast.

When advertising theorist Jib Fowles coined the term chronocentrism in 1974, as 'the belief that one's own times are paramount, that other periods pale in comparison' (Fowles, 1974), I'm sure he did so with the sense that the 1970s were pretty nuts.

We'd just landed on the moon, we'd made Concorde and the Boeing 747, and then faced the global oil crisis. The 1970s saw both economic struggle and vast cultural change. The decade saw the rise of the civil rights movement, a move away from government to the private sector to solve societal and industrial problems, and the rise of individualism. But in retrospect it was nothing compared with now. Right?

The world seems utterly fascinating these days. It seems the pace of change accelerates, fads spread and fade faster than ever, technology is creating profound new possibilities and problems, and we're at some form of tipping point in many different spectrums at the same time.

When I first wrote *Digital Darwinism,* it was driven primarily by a growing fear that we were missing a trick. I felt that the events I attended, the conversations I took part in and the articles I'd devour didn't seem as fascinating as the world did. It seemed we were distracted by exciting irrelevances; we were full of gentle consensus, polite agreement, facile questions, buzzwords, but more than anything else, people were saying a lot of nonsense. Over several hours on a typical day we may have heard that 'drones will change everything', that 'voice will take over search', that 'brands are dying', and those statements generated sufficient frustration and a sense that I could offer thoughts interesting and useful enough to take up a reader's valuable time, to drive me to write my first book.

Driven by this frustration, tempered by a useful amount of self-doubt, I wanted to explore the changes that mattered in the world and to ask new questions, questions I hoped would lead to more interesting conversations and inspire companies to change. I hoped to see change in context, to cover what was changing and what wasn't, to look back on the past to learn and to shift our focus to the future, and to drive bold thinking, optimism and change now.

Four years later and the goal of this totally rewritten book has evolved. I'm here to be more helpful but perhaps less interesting.

To be more directly relevant. I use knowledge from recent years to articulate a clearer journey ahead. My goal is to now provide clarity through moments that seem utterly confusing by stepping back. It's to ask bold, provocative questions about the meaning of technology and how we can rethink around altered assumptions. It's to cast aside the continued utter nonsense we're surrounded by and provide far more concrete, confident, precise guidance on how to get companies to change, because they are still not.

## Let's get liminal

I firmly believe we are at a liminal moment in history. Society is at a threshold between a digitally augmented world and a digitally transformed one. As a species we've evolved over millennia for a world that is local and linear, based on rich interpersonal communication, with scarcity our greatest fear. Collectively over centuries we've developed (locally) etiquette, systems and social norms, and we've planned lives based on rigid shared assumptions about what a good life is. We've had work to tire us out, religion to give us meaning and ritual.

And yet by 2019 it appeared that much of our human wiring, our government policies, our shared sense of etiquette, our assumptions of the world seemed like imperfect foundations and structure for a world that was global, immediate, new, and faced different challenges.

By 2020 we had grown concerned about how much time we were spending on screens, anxious that our children were becoming strangers to reality and evolving to a digital-first world. Loneliness seemed rampant, true connections seemed harder than ever to forge. Above all else we went from a lack of information to a lack of information that we can trust.

We saw the rise of populism and distrust in media, alongside distrust in politicians and, more broadly, 'experts'. We saw countries around the world fracture and divide into smaller units. Power became devolved. Decentralization has become the term du jour. An internet that was supposed to spread empathy, destroy ignorance, empower and connect people, seemed to be having the opposite effect. News and content were first placed online for free, and then written specifically for the age of the algorithmic feed, monetizing attention and then outrage and further dividing the world. Fears of censorship, the rise of cancel culture and then across the world identity politics seemed like new ways of making sense of a complex reality, and the energy of a seemingly chaotic world.

And yet the world was stable. We saw below-normal deaths from terrorism or global wars, steady GDP growth across the planet, generally low and declining unemployment, rising consumer confidence, improved life expectancy and ultra-low interest rates. How could our feelings about the world and reality be so at odds?

By March 2020 that question was muted; the global SARS Covid-19 pandemic and resulting lockdowns created an economic and health shock that boomed around the world. An event that added pressure so precisely on every single key existing societal, political, economic and technological faultline, it almost felt like the act of a genius scriptwriter. Just as distrust in the media, experts, politicians and each other felt overwhelming, we had a virus that tested these vulnerabilities to the extreme. Just as censorship was a growing concern at a time of political and health turmoil, we were asked to wear masks. Whoever writes the script to 'Mankind the series' could not have found a more apt metaphor. Countries retreated to national and regional boundaries, the world felt smaller and more local than it ever had. We were asked to stay inside, to live a virtual existence where loneliness and our ability to connect were tested like never before.

The mesmerizing irony of something so tiny, simple, organic and ancient, bringing to its knees the most sophisticated systems and nations ever known, seemed poetically astonishing. Again, credit goes to the writers.

For many the Covid-19 pandemic has blurred our sense of time and space. Space seems more important than ever around us, and less important than ever to our social circles and relationships in a Zoom-powered world. Time seems to stop and start, bend and blur; days of the week, hours of the day, all seem removed from our normal cadence and marking of time. We're both in a suspended reality and facing a choice of which reality to create.

We've now spent more time apart than we ever expected, and the wealthiest folk on the planet, with the largest homes you can imagine, the greatest power you can hope for, with the means to do whatever they could ever dream of with their time and freedom, have decided it's best to escape it either in a rocket or behind a VR headset. We are suffering from a distinct lack of imagination and ambition. Except in art of course, where greed, FOMO, dubious tastes, poor judgement and free printed money have allowed the marketplace for non-fungible tokens (NFTs) to swell beyond any logic. I can't wait to read this when this is in the past.

As such, life in 2021 feels especially fractious and, well, strange and illogical. Wealth inequality has so far been turbocharged, all while we've never seen or spoken more about a need to ensure fairness. The enthusiasm for a digitally powered and centred life has been proven relentless, at the same time as others have embraced more simple, stoic, real pleasures. We're thrilled by how much extra time we can spend with our kids, and distraught at seeing them kept away from friends. This was a pause perhaps we all needed, but have we learned enough to know what future we should aim to build? Did we do enough deep thinking to contemplate what matters in life, how to best use technology to improve the richness and pleasure of life, without letting it become our master?

The Covid-19 pandemic has forced us to extract ourselves from the muscle memory of everyday life. It could be what we all didn't want, but needed; it's created a reason to change and an excuse to. Nothing focuses the mind quite like necessity. But perhaps it's urgency that is the mother of all invention.

We are at one of the most vital thresholds in all of human civilization. We get the choice between two stark realities: we can seek to return to normal and rebuild what we had, or use this moment to rethink what we decide to return to. We can start without the assumptions of the past, or we can get to reimagine all aspects of our lives. We can challenge the idea of full-time work, of our value being linked to place and time, and instead focus on what value we actually have, not proxies for it.

We now get to focus on the meaning of technology and the implications of it all. We now get to focus on what problems to solve and what new opportunities to work around; we don't need to be distracted by what is next, be it 5G, AI or IoT.

We have all we need right now. We can be confident that all the core tools we could ever need are with us. The Covid-19 pandemic has realistically thrust us into an entirely unexpected but inevitable and easily predicted future. Change is really the construction of a new way. Let's use the feelings of now, the excuse of now, the technology of now and a sense of bold enthusiasm to make a difference. We have everything we need, and yet all we have is now.

## Learning from failure

Throughout this book I have placed several case studies of companies that tried and failed. This must seem like a rather miserable idea. Surely we should seek to be inspired and learn from the great success stories of the world. There are a couple of good reasons for this.

Failure is the best teacher. Many of these companies went about things in an almost exemplary way; they followed almost all known best practice, in many cases took significant risks, acted well before they had to, and used imagination and leadership to make great progress. In each and every case there will be a different specific lesson or two to draw.

It is de rigueur to regale the winners of our time. We are to learn from Jeff Bezos at Amazon that we should seek to celebrate losses as it shows enormous ambition and then one day we will get large enough to be able to cash in on market dominance and be enormously profitable. We should see Uber as a sign we should always play in the grey area of the law and get big enough fast enough to employ top lawyers and win public hearts. The only problem with all this is that success stories are the narratives of the freak exceptions, they are codified and calcified survivorship bias. They are glorified retrospective narratives told in ways that seem logical by the winners of history. Perhaps Amazon was the one success in a field where 100 other companies failed – perhaps it was down to luck? Perhaps some of these people are less 'charismatic visionaries' and more sociopaths whose histrionics we'd do well not to worship. What if a lot of the stories of success we champion are really products of having family money, great connections, a safety net that affords risk taking and the charisma and confidence of a privileged upbringing, and perhaps not wholly attributed to talent, drive, work ethic or genius. The array of direct-to-consumer lifestyle brands launched by ex-Goldman Sachs workers who discovered a love of alpaca wool on a long vacation in Peru, and blazed a trail into fashion, these days has almost become uniform.

## CHAPTER ONE

# Business in the age of disruption

## I wouldn't start from here

There is a tale about a man who, lost in the deepest country lanes of rural Ireland, approaches a passer-by herding sheep along the single-track lane. Winding down the window of his car, the man asks for directions to Dublin. The local takes a deep breath and thinks long and hard before replying, 'Well sir, if I were you, I wouldn't start from here.'

It's not the best joke, but it's a reasonable metaphor for business today. When faced with the winds of change, many of us now feel a sense of regret, saddled with a legacy of what were well-intentioned, well-informed and reasonable decisions but which now, in retrospect, feel unwise. Years and years of tweaks, of new initiatives and seemingly constant course correction have calcified. Years of adding new staff, building new departments and creating more complex structures have merely added complexity and bureaucracy. The resulting cumulative effect is that many businesses are simply not fit to compete with the thrusting insurgent startups that are celebrated in the modern era. With no clear sign of a path ahead, with envy as unicorns (tech companies worth over $1bn) are minted each and every month, yet held to account by different metrics of success, I wonder how many businesses wish they could start from somewhere else?

But increasingly a better question is 'where is the best place to start from?'

If you wanted to build a bank for the future that would best serve customers and make money, would you rather start with a trusted brand, a dominant network of branches around high-traffic areas, deep expertise, relationships with powerful figures in government and regulatory bodies, or would you start with a new core banking system, a challenger brand and vast sums of cash on hand from investors?

If you wanted to build a car company to thrive in the age of electric propulsion, would you rather be a legacy company with factories around the world that have perfected assembly, incredible R&D departments, a network of dealerships to offer repairs, deep partnerships with suppliers but no charging network and limited passion for change, or would you rather be a newcomer like Tesla, Rivian or Lucid, with brilliant new thinking, piles of cash from investors, a powerful narrative in the media, wonderful software engineers, the ability to sell direct to consumers, but concerns over mechanical failures or a chequered history of production?

In recent history, terms like legacy businesses or incumbents have become tainted by an environment that loves to celebrate the dominant stories of success, the incredible stock market valuations and the rapid ascent to stardom. But a key question as the digital age matures is, what is the best place to come from? And this raises questions: do we best thrive by adding innovation constantly at the edges, do we seek to build our future entity from scratch and move to it, or is there a way to transform so deeply and profoundly that we can leverage the best of both? Can we utilize relationships, hard build brands, trust and expertise at the same time as unleashing the power of new technology for an altered consumer marketplace, and start to change how we perceive winners in this space?

This is the key question this book aims to answer: what is the best route for you?

## Understanding how we got here

There is a huge distinction between situations that are *explainable* and those that are *excusable*. The entire modern US Government is a legacy of complex changes, anachronistic decisions and political compromises that make little sense today, but can be explained. The electoral colleges exist as a circuit breaker because the assumption is that the population is too badly informed. States like Maine and Nebraska assign votes in totally different ways to other states. Each state has vastly complex and different voting rules and regulations and they use totally different techniques. The inauguration of a new president still takes place some 72 to 78 days after voting, because it used to take that long for all the votes to come back to Washington to be counted. It was moved forward from double this time period in 1937 because technology had improved. One can easily explain this, but when a nation so proudly defines itself as the world's greatest democracy, it's not easy to excuse it.

The roots of the most modern inventions are firmly constructed on legacy systems, thinking and constraints. That roads (and then cars) were constructed on the paths once rutted by Roman horse-drawn chariots, that the width of the first train container carriages copied automobile car sizes to limit changes required in manufacturing, and that the NASA-designed booster for space missions was contained by a need to fit on a train carriage, does illustrate the perhaps untrue but illuminating idea that a horse's hip size relates to spaceship design. Of course, unlike poor governance, this is both explainable and excusable.

We may think that the fractures in modern society, and the palpable tension that builds around us, are down to a faster-changing world, but we should entertain the idea that they are caused by us seeking to build the future on the foundations of the past.

Companies, like people, are aggregations of all the decisions ever made. They are the result of years of accumulating employees, acquiring businesses, inheriting assets, systems, cultures. For many years the pace of change was sufficiently slow, the fundamental rules of business didn't change, and high barriers to entry were common. We've grown up in an age where being large was a big advantage and where these complex, lumbering beasts could adapt over time. Yet recently, this has totally changed. For years companies ensured they kept their eyes on their closest competitors, which have always been a variety of companies, of significant size, showing clear similarities and demonstrating growth. But now companies face asymmetric competition from fast-growing companies that look nothing like them. Walmart faces endless threats from Amazon, a payments company like Mastercard is forced to compete with a digital wallet like Venmo or a digital payment layer like Klarna. Often the threat is even more unclear. Is Uber a threat to Honda's business model because fewer people require cars? Is Facebook a threat to the *Daily Mail* because people can get their news online? Are Chinese toy companies going to make human-carrying drones and take on large aircraft makers? Will they disrupt fireworks makers too? Does Zoom now threaten large office owners? It's fascinating. As technology companies have grown so quickly, so dramatically, unlimited by national boundaries and often skirting regulations, they've changed the light in which older, more experienced, often larger, legacy companies are viewed. The rapid and famous success of companies like Facebook, Amazon and Google, reaching scale and in some cases profitability in record time, means in some ways that financial markets have become attracted to stocks that offer the promise of explosive valuation growth and view reliable, sturdy, low-growth firms that pay dividends with a sense of FOMO (Fear of Missing Out).

There is a general sense in the world that most battles for the future are between legacy companies and 'tech startups'. There is a clumsy assumption that companies can only ever offer one distinct core competency, and most competition will come down to the simple question, 'Can Tech Company Y get better at understanding and dominating the category Company Z is in than Company Z can understand and then leverage Technology like Y?' It's a simplistic, false narrative, but one that drives the enormous sense of anxiety and change in the modern workplace. Can Monzo get better at banking, or does HSBC need to get better at tech? Can Tesla get better at making cars at scale before VW gets better at battery and software tech? Do the software skills of Carvana allow it to take on CarMax?

For a while the trend lines were very clear. Amazon's skills in technology allowed them to eat retailers alive. Netflix showed that tech people could make or commission great 'TV' far faster than TV companies could learn distribution models (and could secure fresh global rights allowing them to expand voraciously). Facebook got better at selling ads than media owners did at technology, or at least building a digital user base in the modern era. As such there is a growing sense that every technology-based company is destined to own the future. There is an assumption that a direct-to-consumer, tech-driven brand like Harry's can threaten P&G, that Airbnb will undermine and destroy Marriot, or Peloton will eat Equinox. I tend to believe the idea that tech-centric, fast-growing, eager insurgents are bound to dominate is unlikely, but to some extent this isn't the point. The fact is that the fastest-growing and largest companies the world has ever known, like Apple, Facebook, Google, Tesla and Amazon, place enormous, often unfair, pressure to change on every single company on the planet. CEOs, CCOs and CMs of traditional, steady, profit-driving businesses are now made to look sloppy, naïve and unambitious compared with teenagers with hockey stick graphs in investor decks and no idea of what they don't know.

## Altered business rules

The global pandemic caused by SARS Covid-19 has demonstrated the volatility and fragility of the world, and the degree to which significant change can sweep across the planet in ways we've previously considered unimaginable. Large companies have generally been constructed for a world where scale, stability, reliability and depth of knowledge have been proven pillars of success, but in a rapidly changing, unpredictable macro-environment, these increasingly seem like impediments to agility, like energy-sucking bureaucracy and inertia. There are remarkably scant examples of leading legacy companies that have become more adaptable or nimble in a time where consumer expectations, behaviours and the business environment can change so fast.

Big has always been seen to be best. Dominance came from might, not decisiveness or generally even genius. Robust, reliable deployment has traditionally beaten wild, imaginative thinking. Stock markets were created to collect the vast capital required for the construction of railways, big companies gained stability from dominance, assets were intrinsically linked to market capture, and the inherent intrinsic value of purchased assets provided comfort. That is until automotive vehicles were invented. In the same way that there are fundamental laws of nature like gravity, friction or inertia, there have been long-standing laws of business. We knew that larger scale in production tends to reduce costs, that distribution is a vital element to grow, and that depth of knowledge and experience are vital to long-term success. Over the years, best practice gets defined and refined and helps companies improve, often via lower product variance and higher quality of production.

For years we've unquestionably assumed that profit is a great way to raise capital, that a company exists to satisfy consumers, not simply be acquired by an incumbent. We think ideas and expertise and proficiency matter, but now self-belief and audacity seem more important. The internet hasn't changed everything;

it's not smashed every rule of business. But to an alarming degree the fundamentals that companies have long bench-marked against and we've assumed to be constant, and that the advice of large management consultancies has been based on, have drastically altered overnight. When Airbnb is worth more than the five largest hotel companies combined, despite owning no assets, when digital wallets end up with more deposits than banks, or Tesla can be worth more than nine of the largest car companies globally, despite making less than 1 per cent of cars each year, some laws of business *have* to be questioned. It's almost like the physics of the world has been bent then contorted so much, it's not that we now follow the new rules, it's that we don't know what to believe any more. Any storied CFO with a history of managing cashflow and balance books can't help but be perplexed that their competitors seem to get more and more valuable the more they need cashflow to stay afloat, and the more cash they get, the more likely cash will be easier to raise in the future.

What companies have long assumed to be assets are increasingly moving to become less helpful and then actively unhelpful, making changes of any nature far harder.

## Blurred lines

You are what you repeatedly do and make money from, which for many companies has been a clearly defined sector. If you design and manufacture cars, you are an automobile company. If people ask you to store their money for you, you are a bank. If you operate hotels around the world, you are a hotelier. If you make money from selling advertising space, you are a media owner. If you turn tobacco into cigarettes, you are a cigarette maker.

Until around the year 2000 these lines were clear; companies tended to focus on one sector, and would often strive for vertical integration to increase control, reduce dependencies and improve profit margins. One can argue that Harley-Davidson moved to be more of a consumer lifestyle brand than just an iconic motorcycle maker, or that General Motors starting OnStar as a service in 2007 was a shift towards ownership experience, but by and large, lines were easily observed and defined the edges and limitations, providing companies with clear focus on what to do, who their competitors were and what expertise was required.

The explosive growth of eBay in 1995 was perhaps the first example of lines blurring. eBay sold goods in the same way a department store would, but with no inventory, no buyers, remarkably few employees and offering no logistics of its own. It could offer products from cars to clothes, art to electronics, antiques to construction supplies, and even, in the case of Ian Usher, a recently divorced Brit looking for a total lifestyle change, an 'entire life' with a home, car, jet ski, skydiving gear, and his job at a rug store (Reuters, 2008). Since this wasn't a retailer it didn't need to collect taxes, and it could avoid taking responsibility for faulty products as it was just 'a marketplace'.

When PayPal launched around 2000 and Skype launched in 2003, they both raised questions about what exactly they were. Skype was a phone service, but without any network, or hardware, and offering calls for free over the internet. PayPal was a place that offered free transactions, but also held deposits; it was neither a bank account nor a payment processor. These are not just philosophical dilemmas. They are genuine challenges to regulations around the world that have long been built for the clearly defined categories of the past.

Even companies that could be closely defined in terms of old-world sectors were challenging the rules of business. Wikipedia was an online encyclopedia that was both free to access and created entirely by volunteers. Yelp was rather like the Yellow Pages, but businesses didn't pay to list, and it was based on a crowd-generated review system. Netflix started as a movie rental business just like Blockbuster, but there were no late fees and no stores. Everything we thought we knew was being challenged.

We're now in a modern world where few of the descriptions we've used to understand market sectors make sense. Is Airbnb an accommodation provider? Is Uber a taxi company? Is Facebook a media owner? Is Zillow a real estate agency? Is e-cigarette maker Juul a tobacco company, despite making nicotine synthetically and having nothing to do with the tobacco plant?

From Instacart to Ocado to Venmo or Klarna, we have companies that use the understood categories of the past to describe themselves but compete with legacy companies by being so different that lines blur.

The way we've resolved this until now is to simply call them all technology companies. It's helped create a sense of order in an otherwise mystifying world, but more than this, it's allowed companies to enjoy inflated valuations and explain away poor profitability.

But we now ask, so what is a bank? What is a department store? What is a magazine? What is a TV show? What is a record label? What are the defining characteristics of a university, a degree? Bitcoin raises the question, what is money? Netflix makes us ponder, what is the line between a great TV drama and a movie? Podcasts blur the lines of radio. Nike's move to direct commerce blurs the lines of clothing manufacture and retailing. We realize how unclear the world is.

What we really see is an ongoing march to own the customer interface. What we've seen is companies go from vertical players to horizontal ones. Google wants to be the way that people across the entire world find and buy anything, be that from Google Search, or Google Maps, or Google Assistant. Uber wants to be the customer-facing logistics player for getting around town by car, by helicopter or for ordering food. Spotify wants to own music streaming, then podcasts, and perhaps soon TV content. Companies want to spread as wide as they can and be as thin as they can. WeWork wants to operate offices around the world but not own them. Oyo wants to be the largest hotel chain in the world, but to simply provide branding and technical infrastructure, not staff or capital. It's the horizontalization of business, the blurred lines that once defined your industry, business model and provided focus and a lens for competitive threats, which perhaps have contributed to the greatest sense of anxiety to the modern business leader. It is no surprise that industries like mining, energy, utilities, airlines, telecommunications or construction, where value is intrinsically linked to tangible items, face a calmer moment.

## Regulatory hacking

Regulations have been designed for a vertical world. The FTC antitrust commission is happy to stop Harry's being purchased by Edgewell, the parent company to Schick and Wilkinson Sword, fearful that they'd be too powerful by owning 15 per cent of the wet shave market (Del Rey, 2020). Yet Amazon was allowed to buy Pillpack, Wholefoods and Zappos to have up to 50 per cent of the US e-commerce market (Sheeler, 2021). Netflix is fine with 36.2 per cent of the streaming market share (Brumley, 2021), and Google is fine with 91 per cent of search and 37 per cent of digital advertising spending (Proceed Innovative, 2021). These examples provide a strong sense of the ambiguity and unfairness in the modern world. How do we know what market Amazon belongs to? Is its share a share of all commerce in the United States? Should it be just e-commerce? What exactly is e-commerce? Google has 91 per cent of search but what industry is that?

For years large companies, with assets acting as liabilities, shareholders to hold them to account, enduring powerful brands that could be tarnished immediately and lawyers employed to safeguard their interests, have used regulation as clear warning lines to keep clear of. Any meeting with a bank, pharmaceutical company, car maker or even telecommunications company would be regularly punctuated with 'well we can't do that, we're highly regulated'. Uttering 'regulation' was enough to excuse anything.

Startups, looking only at the potential of growth, and with nothing to lose and no potential damage, view regulations as grey areas to exploit. Lyft first hacked the taxi industry by insisting that it wasn't a taxi company because payments were merely suggested donations. Uber gained further ground by positioning itself as part of the 'sharing economy'; this way drivers were simply people with spare time and a spare car. They didn't need to be employed, didn't need worker protection, cars didn't need to be checked for safety standards, and all Uber was was a marketplace matching needs to solutions. Being a marketplace thanks to Section 230 of the US Code enacted as part of the United States Communications Decency Act of 1996 generally provides immunity from liability for providers and users of an 'interactive computer service' who publish information provided by third-party users. AKA we're just a marketplace, nothing is our fault.

Airbnb also rode the wave of sharing, now offering hosts a chance to dabble around the edges of zoning laws, circumvent a few safety laws, be a little vague on tourist taxation, and could avoid many of the responsibilities faced by the hotel chains they competed with. It is after all merely a marketplace.

Facebook, Twitter, LinkedIn or Instagram can monetize content, but not be responsible for fact-checking or fraudulent goods or drugs sold, or for showing acts of violence – it's just a platform. Increasingly this is now facing pressure from governments and the future looks, well, complicated.

Tesla was able to circumvent laws that ban direct manufacturer auto sales on the basis that their cars were good for the world, and that existing franchises may not work hard enough to sell them and may be unable to explain to their customers the advantages their cars have over traditional combustion engines. Even in states like Texas which still ban direct sales for Tesla,

Tesla simply operates retail stores but asks customers to complete purchases over the phone to someone out of state or on the internet. Connecticut also banned direct sales, but Tesla bypasses this law by leasing out cars (Scinto, 2020).

These complexities are becoming more pervasive than ever. In June 2016, when Democrats in the US Congress were trying to force a vote on gun control legislation, Republican Paul Ryan forced TV cameras to turn off, assuming that would draw a veil over what was happening; but instead two protesting representatives turned on their phones and broadcast proceedings in near-perfect quality over Facebook and Periscope, to ironically a potentially much larger audience (Lerner, 2016). TV cameras are easy to ban but there are no such rules in place for streaming, and what does streaming even mean?

Bird became one of the fastest unicorns ever with its electric scooters, growing in 14 months to launch in 120 cities, to now be worth $2 billion (Yakowicz, 2019). Yet this is a company rooted in letting people rent electric scooters when, in most cities in which they operate, it's illegal for people to ride them on the road, and illegal on pavements. It's become clear that the Silicon Valley mantra of 'move fast and break things' could sometimes include the law. The hope is that companies can be small enough to be unnoticed, then grow fast enough to become too big to take on.

How can large companies deal with this? Playing to the rules seems a little unfair.

## Investor demands

We've seen thrusting insurgent companies built for the modern age change the market. We've observed the rise of companies that have ignored all known wisdom. They have built themselves with the latest technology at their core; they have skirted round or ignored prior regulations and bent the rules. They are constructed on new economic principles and counter-intuitive business models that have treated legal and societal responsibility as externalities. These companies often have lower operating costs, scale fast, and have often removed value from entire markets. These have been companies held to account by metrics like user growth, not revenue, by monthly users, not profit. These are companies for which generating profit is assumed to be a lack of ambition, where all funds should be ploughed into relentless growth across demographics, regions and categories. It's these companies, valued more highly than at almost any other time, despite often being intrinsically unprofitable, that legacy companies are not just compared with but are expected to emulate somehow. It's companies with new thinking, new expectations, new cultures and with the latest technology embedded deeply at the very core of their business that seem to offer the best structure for growth in the future.

And so we've seen investing start to split. There are stocks like Airbnb which can pop on IPO by 113 per cent, or DoorDash which shot up 86 per cent (Kim, 2020), or Snowflake, the cloud-based data management company rising 112 per cent in a day (Pressman, 2020). And then there are stocks like P&G or Unilever, which have taken 20 years to double in value, or Samsonite or Coty or Revlon, which have lost more than 50 per cent of their value.

Generally speaking, the market has bifurcated into fast-growth, high-return, moderate- to high-risk stock like Uber, WeWork, Stripe, Tesla, Airbnb, Roku, Zillow, Ocado, Redfin, Carvana and Snapchat, and low-growth, low-risk, dividend-paying stocks like BMW, Mondalez, Nestlé, Avis and IWG (formerly Regus). One has to ask the question: do these companies accept the category they are in? If investors in Avis are not expecting high growth but expect low risk, then what is the business case for radical change? If the owners of British American Tobacco stock expect a 10 per cent dividend year on year, do they want this company to reimagine the future of relaxation or just to keep finding new smokers?

The comparison of 'tech company that just happens to make suitcases', like Away with Samsonite, is clear – one makes lots of money and the other is likely experiencing low or no profitability, but valued an inordinately greater amount. Brands like Allbirds now dominate over brands like Skechers, despite being financially weak. It's the cognitive dissonance between companies that are well run and churn out steady profit and revenue growth being made to feel weak while their competitors lose a fortune month on month and state that a lack of profit is a sign of ambition. More than anything else, when traditional profit-making companies that have huge and dependable market share are compared with thrusting upstarts with wildly different price-to-earnings ratios, you can see how a sense of jealousy sets in. It seems that the investor market is bifurcated into reliable, profitable, boring companies that may pay dividends, and wildly exciting growth stocks that could go to the moon. Perhaps pressure should be on the inflated expectations of tech companies but instead it falls on traditional companies to return quarter-on-quarter growth. And yet the requirement for large, incumbent companies to produce steady reliable income with almost zero risk is the most impossible platform for radical innovation to be built on.

## Over-production and marketing-led organizations

For most of human civilization, scarcity has been the greatest problem and the solution was making more stuff. For centuries, we worked hard to produce things for ourselves or in small communities, and it was only during and after the Industrial Revolution that purchasing goods slowly became easier for a consumer than just making things for themselves. Mass production also led to the development of mass media. It created a need for producers to find better ways to develop products, and when products moved from commodities to being differentiated via quality, there was a need for a more sophisticated approach to informing customers about these commodities, and the notion of a brand arose. And thus marketing was born.

It's not that everyone could afford the first TV sets, or the Model T Ford, but it wasn't the case that they were unwanted. After decades where execution had been the focus, and effort was placed entirely on manufacturing efficiency and consistency, the focus shifted to how we could meet demand.

Demand generation is largely a modern construct; the notion of marketing, of listening to consumers, of changing what you make because of what you think they may like, was a much larger shift than we may presume. It's not something companies were made for. And now the world's economy has become globalized, barriers to entry are rapidly diminishing and advertising is becoming more accessible than ever, and the internet allows easy comparison of prices.

## Changing consumer behaviours and expectations

For years, people were more likely to get divorced than change bank account, but now apps like Monzo, Starling or N26 allow for a new account to be opened in less than 15 minutes and a few clicks. For decades, going to the local mall was a rite of passage for kids and department stores were the way to experience an array of products you could not buy elsewhere. For most of our lives, restaurants were chosen based on proximity, yet now the Burger King and McDonald's apps may be less than one inch away from each other on our phones. Things have changed.

The world of search means we can compare prices from seemingly all retailers in seconds. Companies with skeletal staff can construct digital storefronts that look as impressive as real-world stores with thousands of outlets. Loyalty, often based on proximity or the routines of life, now comes down to familiarity or risk aversion or simply the act of letting us buy with one click and not having to get up to find our purse or wallet.

We are now used to companies over-serving us at their cost. Each day, Amazon delivers vast boxes of low-margin goods next day for free – our expectations have changed. When we can see the Uber or Lyft driver's name, real-time location and contact them directly, we are stunned when we get a delivery slot of five hours in the afternoon and no means to talk. We now find the idea of anything ordered arriving days later inept, rather than the reality of a complex global logistics system held hostage by grounded ships in the Suez or global component shortages.

When Netflix offers us some of the best TV ever made for less than a movie ticket, or ClassPass offers us access to millions of gyms for less than our local gym, we start to assume we're being taken for a ride, not that venture capital firms are subsidizing our extravagant demands. Free has become normal for countless brilliant websites featuring content that takes expertise, craft and a fortune to create.

We now expect websites from every company to be beautiful, fast and thoughtful; why can't I pay my rent with a credit card with one touch? Why can't I buy access to my local swimming pool online? Why is there not a map of all electric car charging stations showing empty spaces, and why are there coin-operated parking meters here? We have to accept that loss-making start-ups and vast tech giants have changed how we see every business and interaction we experience.

## Digital inertia

While the world has been changing more rapidly than we have been comfortable with, while new technology has made things possible, while consumers have slowly become used to and then expect the best-in-class experience provided by companies built for the modern age with new technology at the core, large companies have generally changed little.

We live in a moment in time where companies are told to disrupt or die, to be a startup or be left behind; we are told the pace of change is faster than ever, and we live in unprecedented and unpredictable times. And I'm just not sure this is the case.

Perhaps what's really happened is that during decades of a relatively benign global environment with extremely low interest rates, low unemployment, growing economic prosperity, and with quite honestly remarkably few cases of dramatic failure like Kodak, Nokia or Blockbuster, most companies felt little need to really change. We think we live in the golden age of innovation, but really we live in the age of consolidation, share buybacks and high dividends for shareholders. We live with companies doing the least they have to do in order to not fall foul of the financial markets. Realistically, this approach makes sense. The reality is that profound change is hard, requires buy-in across departments, and the business case for change is rarely clear. I'm aware that many senior leaders reading this will be frustrated at what appears to be criticism of inaction, when in fact I merely want to present a clear picture of where we are. Business leaders do an amazing job these days of navigating the stormy and cloudy waters of the modern business world.

Yet each day technology makes new things possible. Each passing week creates a larger delta between the wonder of what is possible and the reality of a company changing slowly or not at all. What we feel isn't so much the chaos of a faster-changing world, but increasing tension, a blockage that's piling up. We see older banking systems become even more outdated, venture capitalists feeling ever more reluctant to look under the hood; we see companies hoping to survive rather than put the effort into opening the can of worms that is the crumbling foundations on which they were constructed.

It's these three changes – rapid global change, the changing physics of business, and the rise of insurgent companies – above all else that now make life different. They mean that companies have to think hard, be bold, be imaginative, audacious and challenge themselves. In this chapter I want to introduce the main concepts of Digital Darwinism, how it can drive and contextualize business transformation, and better address change in the modern post-Covid world. This chapter is about understanding the context and reason for change, while providing a wider foundation for concepts that I build on in later chapters. But more than anything else, I want to get businesses of all shapes, sizes and maturity to start asking the right questions: the hard, existential ones.

## What would your company look like if you set it up today?

This book is designed to appeal to a variety of readers: those working in leadership roles in large companies that need to change but find it hard, those who are working in less instrumental positions and are curious, but also those leading insurgent startups eager to make the most of the opportunities in the world today. It's also designed to make sense of a changing world and be used for our personal lives. In many ways the way we see our lifestyles and the tensions we experience in the chaos of today can be illuminated and informed by some of the questions posed in this book.

It is extremely easy, popular and fashionable to tinker at the edge of companies. In particular in the post-pandemic age, many of the questions about the way we run businesses are based on what appeared to be long-lasting, significant changes but are (or could be) actually rather short-lived or less noteworthy than first appeared.

We end up distracted, focusing on where people work in an age of remote work, or how to best attract diverse talent, rather than daring to ask questions that go to the very core of who we are.

The most profound and the very best questions we never dare to ask are: What would your business look like if it was created today? What would it do? How would it do it? How would it make money? What would you still have done and what would you never have created?

## Do you have to change?

The next questions to ask are: Can you carry on like this? At what point in size or inefficiency does it make sense to go back to the drawing board? Your business may be able to function each day, but for how long will that be the case? We know deep down that one day people will not smoke tobacco, that car makers will need to make electric cars and provide access to charging networks. We know many retailers will need more efficient mechanisms to supply direct online. We know sustainability is a topic that will not go away. We know that oil companies will have to really change to become energy companies at some point, that department stores are a construct of the past, that live TV will crumble under the threat of all manner of more immediate distractions on our phones. To what extent should companies facing demonstrably hopeless futures consider not the investment required to change what they do but the inexorable cost of failure if they don't?

But we forget sometimes that while it's relatively easy to predict what will happen, it's far, far harder to predict when it will happen, or sometimes where.

There are of course many sectors that may not face great change: mining, timber, farming, water provision will of course face change, but probably not to the same level of chaos, threat and opportunity. A key aspect to ponder is, are you genuinely in denial about the change facing your industry? Are you blinkered to the possibilities that could be exploited or are you perhaps destined to do just fine, but have been seduced by consultancies into thinking that Blockchain or NFTs or a startup with terrible unit economics will undermine you?

## What should your future vision be?

This book attempts to summarize many elements of the future that will help us create a platform for growth. If we accept that we work in a dynamic world where many of the aspects of business that used to be very challenging are rather simple, that the barriers to new ventures or models are now vastly reduced, we can start the process of establishing a much healthier foundation for future profitability and expansion. We can look at the core elements of what we do better than anybody else and bring to life and ideate around new territories for the future, but in a way that is aligned to both our strengths and realistic change. We can work hard to envisage our future role in consumers' lives.

## How can you change?

I believe in change through growth and growth through change. How can we shape a new working model, from operations to culture, encompassing structure, processes, policies, procedures and, most importantly, what strategies do we follow to get there?

For those who accept that fundamental change needs to happen, you should ask, what can you do to get to that place? Can you get there with what you have, or do you need to start again? Who and what will help make this happen? How can this realistically be done? I've long held the belief that it's easier to build than it is to change. That rather than digital or cultural transformation, we should focus more on growth. It is the energy, momentum and freedom of growth that best allows companies to change path; muscle memory is strong and change creates resistance, but building anew brings about optimism, confidence and excitement.

## When should you change?

Finally, when do you change? When technology seems to develop more rapidly than ever, is deployed and popularized more quickly each year and then combines in new ways to form new permutations of great meaning, we need to be aware of the right moment in time to jump on the next wave of innovation. In many ways innovation seems like surfing: not only do you need to ignore many waves and choose the best one, you need to time the leap perfectly in order to catch it.

All we have is now, now is all we have.

In order to best answer these questions and to initiate your approach to the changing world and digital transformation, it's essential to look at how technology evolves and to learn from the past, which we explore in Chapter 2.

### ACTION

For some reason we presume that if we are not in the optimal position in life then it means poor decisions have been made, yet often it's because we made great decisions based on all the information available to us at the time. We typically need to remove a sense of regret or blame from any process that involves an honest look at moves or decisions made that turned out to be wrong.

As a good way to exercise these muscles it's worth asking questions like:

- What business or financial decisions have you made that it turns out were wrong?
- What can you do to rectify them?
- What do you learn by evaluating why you made that decision?

CHAPTER TWO

# The three phases of change

*We become what we behold. We shape our tools and then our tools shape us.* OFTEN ATTRIBUTED TO MARSHALL MCLUHAN

There is a slight sense that technology has spread across the world and changed everything. A feeling that we're living in a new digital age, where the foundations of society have moved, where innovation is everywhere and the work has largely been done. We even have a sense we've missed out; if only we'd had a garage in the 1960s, or dropped out of Stanford, we'd be rich, but that moment won't ever arise again. Now we've got Slack on our phones, Amazon, Zoom and Alexa, we can regret the missed opportunities but feel relieved the disruption is over. There is an odd sense that somehow 'everything that can be invented has been invented'.

We are perhaps in the very early stages of some current change not yet fully understood. Perhaps we've barely understood the meaning of a world of cloud-based servers, where screens are thin, cheap, large and internet-connected, or explored the full power of 4G mobile internet, let alone made the most of even more exciting, recent and profound developments in technology – come on, 5G internet must mean something? We can't argue that putting iPads in some classrooms is all that is possible to transform education, or that urban planning rules in the age of the tiny home or 3d printed homes, or Airbnb, are just fine. Getting health insurance in the United States if you dare spend your life in more than one state is challenging. What employment rights do you have if you work for a Californian firm, for a Seattle-based client, but do most of your work in Texas? From democracy to taxation to the welfare state to how we look at the long lives we are likely to all lead, where pensions are designed to take care of our worn-out bodies for a short time before we die – we need to understand the wonderful power to make better things that lie ahead!

## Seeing change in context

The present is always a terrible vantage point from which to approach change in the world. In this chapter I want to go back in time and, by understanding mistakes from the past, learn how best to approach today, or at least offer reasonable explanations for why things may feel like they do.

From around the 1880s onwards and over four decades, electricity spread purposefully and slowly across the world, bringing small incremental changes to factories and homes, but didn't do anything transformative. Most years, these small changes kept factory managers happy and domestic lives seemed to improve nicely. But it's only in retrospect that we can see how the transformative power of electricity was not properly harnessed.

From factory owners to workers, homeowners to retailers, each and every person thought they'd understood this new technology, and thought they'd made the necessary changes. They seemed to treat electricity as a new thing to bolt on to the side, a tweak based on small improvements, never truly digesting the meaning of this technology and working around the new possibilities it offered. It's this paradox of transformative potential vs actual change that should concern everyone, but also empower and reassure others looking to drive change or innovation or be more ambitious in any business today.

## The electrical revolution took time

The key way to think about electricity in the home was that it had many phases. First, an era of people discovering and refining a technology so that it could be used. A period of massive investment in infrastructure, debates about protocols and standards, and new regulations and laws. Then came a period when electricity was something only for the rich, a new trivial toy or fancy folly, with possibilities that were hard to recognize, a period when we added power to old items to marginally improve their functionality. Then finally, several decades in, a period when the technology plummeted in price, became more reliable, far more accessible to all, but above all else, new items were created around the potential of the technology, offering clear benefits. We could even argue a fourth stage appeared after that, where the social, behavioural and commercial implications rather slowly emerged and new rituals, etiquette and habits slowly transpired.

Michael Faraday first began generating power in a consistent, practical way in 1831, and it was not long before the current was reversed and the first electric motor was born. One would expect something that became quite so transformative to have a near-immediate effect on the world, but this was not the case. Much like the early internet, few could see the meaning at the start. (Note, this does not mean that every technology that few can see the meaning of is destined to become significant – I'm looking at you, Blockchain.)

By the late 1800s only a very small percentage of domestic dwellings had electricity. Like most new technology it was first sold to wealthy homes as something of a gadget; first as a better way to light Christmas trees, and then a better way to light homes. In an era when the wealthy employed staff to light candles or gaslights, electricity didn't seem that helpful to them; it made more sense when marketing messages to sell the concept of electricity turned to the safety of it over real flames and later the ability for owners to control devices themselves, directly.

From 1888 we saw Christmas tree lights, heaters, cookers, irons and toasters slowly become electrified, then food mixers, fans, shavers and fridges, but these all replaced preexisting mechanical or chemically based equivalents. All items that, while better than nonelectrified versions, provided no massive leaps forward (with perhaps the exception of the refrigerator). Nobody created anything new around electrical power. Somehow the idea of creating something nobody previously knew could exist, or working around the power of something new, was beyond most human imagination.

It was only after around 1910 that we saw new items made for the environment or possibilities the electricity allowed for, like dishwashers, tumble dryers, vacuum cleaners, electric hair dryers, radios, air conditioning and telephones. It was these that created huge leaps in the lives that we could lead. All items impossible to imagine, let alone want or make, in the pre-electrical age.

The developments were fascinating in how they impacted the world, and as the products became better and cheaper, it was now within the grasp of the middle class to have clean homes, clothes and a better appearance, without hours of domestic work. Yet rather than the amount of time spent doing chores decreasing in an era of far more efficient devices, it's simply changed societal expectations of how clean our clothes should be, how orderly our homes should be, and the time saved has simply passed on to doing household chores more often.

But it's the adoption or failed adoption of electricity in factories that is most useful to illuminate to understand how businesses in the world can transform.

## Electricity in factories

Factories constructed from the 18th century were built around a power system based on a 'line drive shaft', a huge, long, spinning shaft that would directly or indirectly power all the equipment in a factory layout. In the very first factories, this shaft was turned by waterpower, with factories built around steady supplies of decent running water.

The invention of the steam engine in the 18th century at first didn't change much, with pioneering and risk-taking factory owners using it to lift water to drive the same waterwheels and increase the flow and reliability of waterpower – a change the people were very happy about. Slowly it dawned on people that replacing waterwheels with steam engines was a better play. They provided more torque, were more controllable and allowed factories to be constructed anywhere people wished, so long as coal could be easily delivered in large quantities.

The line drive shaft dominated the design of the factory. Factories were constructed as long rectangular shapes, to ensure that all the equipment could pull power from it. Walls were massive and heavy to hold the weight of it. Windows for light or ventilation were impractical.

When electrical motors were invented, the required change was obvious, as a form of power that could offer more torque, could come on stream faster, could be cheaper and more efficient, and required less maintenance; factory owners slowly replaced worn-out steam engines with large electrical motors.

Real change came about by several seemingly different movements coming together. Electricity production became cheaper and far more reliable, distribution improved slowly during the 1920s and '30s, and electrical motors became cheaper and more efficient. They also became much smaller.

It was these factories that were built from scratch, and conceived and constructed with the knowledge of electrical motors and in totally different ways than they would have been had they been built on legacy water- or steam-powered operations. For the first time ever, rather than merely assuming that large drive shafts would be central to factory architectures and processes, designers worked around the machinery and the workflow that best suited the manufacturing process.

Factories were reimagined. Everything known, assumed and fixed was challenged. New factories and designs could be constructed in the context of easy, fast, cheap, abundant energy, the electrical cables infinitely easier to manage than drive shafts.

Layouts of factories could follow the most sensible layouts for the manufacture of goods in the most efficient way. Huge productivity gains, visible from this one change, also reduced the messiness of the flow of goods in one go. Workers suddenly became both trained and empowered; they'd work harder and see the great effects of their responsibility. Factories could remove (or never build) the millwork. There could be windows, so the fire risk was immediately reduced and ventilation improved. The notion of power or energy became not a physical element that drove the layout but the background entity that made anything possible. It was the enabler, not the constraint. Large gearboxes and pulleys were replaced with switches and rheostats.

Freed from the constraints that came from power distribution, activities on the factory floor could be reorganized to bring about much better production arrangements. Factories no longer needed to be elongated with complex flows; they could be any shape the company needed. Buildings could be constructed far more efficiently and multiple floors were now possible.

But by far the biggest shift happened on a macro level. For hundreds of years the location of plants had been dictated by energy needs. At first the need was to locate near reliable fast-running water to power waterwheels, then it was the need to be near coal or near a transportation route that offered easy and cheap access to huge amounts of coal. Energy was never something that could be transported.

This requirement was completely removed by electricity, and for the first time in history factories were free. They could be near sources of employment in large cities, or they could be located near ports where inbound ingredients and products made from them could be transported far more easily.

It turns out that every profound technology has a similar phasal mechanic to its adoption. We don't see specific or niche technologies like the bicycle, iron or typewriter have these phases, but we do see significant, wide, platform-like technologies affect society and business in the same way, from steam to electricity and, in more recent times, computing power and computers themselves.

## Computerization

Before the mainframe was popularized along with desktop work and personal computers, life across business, education, home and transportation had been the same for years. The rituals and patterns of life were set. We had places of work where we gathered together at set times, and where value was created. Education was done in institutions, first linked to the church, then to the armed forces and universities and schools. Place and time were fixed by the need to be synchronously present in one place.

The working day could be extended by commuters on trains taking briefcases to work, and information could be spread further by the use of xerography machines, but communication was limited. It's bizarre to think of an office in this age. What did people do all day? What was on everybody's desk? A world of phone calls made from desks, calendars on paper, memos sent around in envelopes, carbon paper-based copying. In this era, offices were aligned like command-and-control systems replicated from the armed forces with a strict organizational hierarchy, an essential structure when communication takes time and costs money. And with information largely flowing one way – down.

A world of bureaucracy and control, paper trails, forms to fill in and file away, rubber stamping and internal mail protocols. Progress was slow and improvements limited; slightly faster photocopiers, cheaper ink, better workflows, cheaper and more advanced calculators developed at a snail's pace. Desks were lined with in-trays and outboxes. There were no blue screens of death, no 'systems down for maintenance' at weekends, no server issues or hacking or privacy breaches and scandals. I'm certainly not suggesting life was better, but everything worked smoothly and slowly, and there was little doubt about the best way to work.

The advent of computers didn't change business overnight. As with electricity, it took a while, was ignored by many businesses, and adopted with different speeds, enthusiasm and depth by different companies, sectors and nations.

For a start, the capital expenditure seemed extraordinary. Companies would need to shift from spending money on paper, pens and a little labour moving envelopes around, to investing in primitive, huge, massively expensive machines, with limited software, that would only really work if other people used the same devices. And machines that become outdated rapidly and would be worthless in a few years. What sort of accountant would be happy to make this leap of faith with something largely unproven?

New skills would be required; entire workforces would have to be retooled to use this new technology, but would be carrying out very similar jobs. This would not only be expensive but would also lead to new errors, need new policies, require new thinking. Companies would need to employ entirely new staff. The 'IT' function couldn't be upskilled procurement people who'd previously been buying 'technology' like ink, typewriters or mimeograph copying machines, it had to be new people with different knowledge, people who existed in tiny numbers and didn't have much experience. How would you even go about recruiting such people when you didn't know what questions to ask them?

Computers were first used to embellish the existing structures and systems. We bolted on a new IT department, reluctantly and entirely as a support function. What changed was an addition, rather than a replacement for what we had in the past.

Faced with complexity and new things to learn, we replicated the familiar units of the past. We took all the old-world systems and digitized them. Skeuomorphism, the design concept of making digital items resemble their real-world counterparts, was a way to aid the transition into the new era. Mail became e-mail, with addresses and inboxes. We made 'folders' and 'trash' and 'desktops' as digital equivalents. PowerPoint had 'slides' like early slide projectors and floppy disks represented 'saving', which is wonderfully anachronistic, as is 'return', which stands for 'carriage return' from typewriters – and don't even start me on 'cc' for carbon copy.

Yet at the same time, businesses stuck to the order, tempo and methodologies of the past. Despite the adoption of desktop and laptop computers, almost everything remained the same. In-person meetings were required, weekly status calls were held, recruitment used the same template to attract and filter potential employees, corporate organization charts stayed the same. What was once a faxed-in handwritten weekly sales report became an Excel spreadsheet emailed at the same time. What was a sales presentation delivered with images and diagrams became the same with PowerPoint slides.

We first printed out emails, and we kept internal mail to send them around, even as mail became electronic. We worked in offices where some kept paper calendars, others their own personal digital calendar, while more people slowly used collaborative digital calendars.

Desktop computers have changed the need for briefcases and intranets changed the need for libraries, but computing has changed remarkably little of the way that we go about our work. Laptops and then mobile phones have done far less to improve efficiency, and instead have just extended the working day and made the office the entire world. The paperless office of the future never appeared. We still fill in an inordinate amount of forms by hand, we still need wet signatures on some documents, and we send the very most important things, like passports, car titles or ID cards, by mail.

## Learning from the history of technology adoption

People think they've got it when they haven't. For years the owners of factories thought they had used electrical technology to the best of its capability and done all they needed to do. In fact they'd hardly touched the surface. There is always a sense of false start, a fear that we've missed a trick – we think each time it's different.

We see that economics gets in the way of anything new, or investing in anything that makes things happen that we can't imagine yet. The business case for significant change, especially around anything new, is hard. It's a lethal combination of unknown, unpredictable benefits that are hard to quantify, and the significant cost of real change, prone to great variance and considered noncritical.

Muscle memory is strong; organizations are built for routine and repetition and continuous linear improvement within a mindset. Asking people to think differently or create something truly new is very hard, especially with people with experience and expertise in the current way of doing something.

When we face something new we find it hard to really rethink. We can't start with a blank sheet of paper to create a vision of something we should create. It seems the starting point for any innovation is the memories of everything that we know to already exist. In order to feel more in control, we excitedly and rapidly attach it to what we understand. Most innovation is a remix of a remix; it becomes circular, iterative and recursive, optimizing based on assumed inputs and parameters.

Change needs to be deep. We tend to want to apply new technology as a way to lubricate existing systems. Often deep down it appears we favour dealing with new technology as a threat to digest and prove to the world we understand, more than a transformative power that may require a lot of effort to work around. To rethink things from the core level takes huge political will and also requires a lot of imagination and risk. Timescales and business plans in business favour fast, cheap and immediate payback. It was when electric motors got small, and computer chips became abundant and cheap, making connectivity a given, that things really changed.

We have no ability to imagine things that have never happened before. It is simply impossible to calculate the benefits of something that has never been done before. Companies are focused maniacally on the past, case studies, best practices and an array of backwards-facing mechanisms.

Timing is vital. Technology is always changing what is possible and knowing the right time to invest in a new system is key. We assume fast is good, that first to market wins, but from Webvan to Friends Reunited to Myspace to the Palm Pilot, or those companies which invested in owning their own servers as the world moved to cloud computing, being too early is very much being wrong. In fact, most companies moving too early tend to act rather like snow ploughs or icebreakers; they use enormous energy to clear the way (regulations, required behaviour changes, unassailable business problems), letting those behind forge a path with less danger and energy.

Things take longer than you think. Rather like we currently think the modern world has been transformed by digital, we should be aware that change requires much longer than we think, typically three to four decades. To assume that things are faster than ever and there is nothing new under the sun shows a lack of understanding of how slowly humans and society often change.

And more than anything it's companies that are newly built for the age that unleash the real power of a new technology. The invention of the mechanical elevator didn't change any existing building, it transformed new buildings designed for a world where people could effortlessly reach higher floors, propelling buildings into the sky. The car had a far greater impact on cities like Los Angeles, Detroit or Miami, which largely flourished after their invention, than older cities like New York or London. Large companies have not been the first to switch to electric propulsion; it is neobanks that are building their new core banking systems around new software, not larger ones. Change is very hard. The number of companies which have rethought themselves, integrated new technology or developed new cultures is remarkably small. It's not the case that companies need to start from zero to thrive, but it's notable in history that it was new devices made for the world of electricity, or new factories built around new motors, or companies harnessing the power of computing at the core, that have always propelled the world to new places.

### ACTION

Think of an industry that seems to have already changed a lot due to digital technology and try to imagine all the ways it could really be reimagined if we were more ambitious and could make amazing things happen and worked around the parameters of the modern era.

Stuck for ideas? How about the retirement business, or home construction, or welfare benefits, or the tax code, or the process of buying a house, or try something boring like health insurance or shopping malls.

What we see with the examples of electricity and computing power is also demonstrated by a whole array of technologies. By no means do all technologies follow the same pattern. The adoption curves are linked to the profoundness in meaning of a new technology, not the degree of complexity or sophistication.

It was the humble shipping container that changed world trade for ever, but only when systems, ports, trucks and ships were first converted and then built from scratch to work around them. What first appeared to be a quirky idea soon became a revolution that affected the entire global economy.

The invention of the car at first seemed like a very expensive horse, before enthusiastic adoption ended up changing the way that cities and homes were designed; again, existing cities that modified their appearance to fit cars ended up radically different and less car-efficient than the new cities constructed around the power of the car.

This adoption curve is seen from barbed wire changing the way the entire unsettled Midwest of America was colonized, leading to vast gains in productive land and huge social change, to the telephone, which required the network effect, ie having someone with a phone to call.

It often seems that the most boring technology can allow the world to be radically altered, but only if its adoption takes off, and only if the meaning of the technology is then worked around, which becomes a reinforcing cycle.

In an age where we celebrate Blockchain or NFTs or 3D printing, we give little thought to the amazing power of inventions like the passport or batteries or plastic or copyright protection or property deeds. From steel to contraceptives, nails to the microwave, the Gregorian calendar to the alphabet, the camera to petrol, we often forget how rudimentary innovation can be transformative.

Even now, often when I'm asked to name some of the most profound technologies around, the assumption is that I will mention drones or graphene, when I really believe it's developments in batteries, modular homes, QR codes and LEDs that could totally change much of modern life, but only if we go about the process of working around their potential.

## The three phases of technology

All new, profound technology ostensibly follows a path of three phases:

1 First, we have a pre-technology environment, before the new technology is discovered or used in any way. In this period things generally are understood, the pace of change is slow, and improvements are incremental. In this environment best practice is key, companies know how to make money, and the world seems stable and understood. This is the world of shipping before the container, the world of TV before cable, the canal industry before the steam age, the record industry before the MP3, the banking sector before the credit card, or bookselling before the internet.

2 Then a new technology or way of thinking with the potential to change everything is installed or disseminated. This happens around existing mindsets and processes, augmenting and lubricating what went before. At this stage we have both the new and the old, with competing systems, inherited protocols, the feeling of change and panic; it's where we often live with the most confusion and uncertainty. This often means peak complexity. A world where Macs and PCs don't work with each other, or AC and DC currents exist, or USB B, Mini USB and USB C adaptors clutter our homes. In this stage land grabs appear, little money is made by most, and the world feels utterly tumultuous but exciting.

3 And then we have a third phase where we make sense of the new technology, where systems are rebuilt for the new world. It is in this final stage, when society and the commercial world appear to have made sense of the change, that the technology moves to the background and is widely understood and built upon. It's in this final stage that things appear simply to work. We no longer think about dialling up to get the internet or

going online; we live in a digitally augmented world with no line. We no longer deal with PAL, SECAM or NTSC TV formats, or VHS vs LaserDisc vs DVDs for movies. It's this final stage where the winners start to win big.

## The awkward middle age of technology

The furniture in our living room has gone from being oriented around the fireplace to being focused on the TV set, but in the area where most consumption now happens on mobile devices, we are in a moment of extremely subtle chaos. Such is the complexity of the way the technology changes our lives.

The hybrid car is another perfect example of mid-technology complexity. A combustion-propelled car is mechanically complex, with thousands of moving parts, but has been optimized to be incredibly efficient, pretty cheap to buy, well understood, with mechanics all over the world well-tooled to fix it. Electric cars, powered by enormous batteries, offer wildly new opportunities for new designs, have incredible performance (with radical acceleration and amazing efficiency) and drastically reduce the number of moving parts, with far cheaper maintenance and much easier manufacturing.

But around 1997, led by Toyota, before electric cars were economically viable, we saw the hybrid car. A car with all the complexity of a gasoline-powered car, and all the complexity of an electric car combined in one. A perfectly good combustion vehicle, with a small battery, generative braking, electric motors and their costs added to it. A car offering almost none of the benefits of electric cars, nor combustion cars, with plenty of the drawbacks of both, but it was about 20 per cent more efficient and was seen as great progress (Phys.org, 2006).

At any moment in time some elements of life are getting more complicated and some are getting more simple. Buying flights is simpler, buying train tickets more complex. Macs now seem happy to .talk to PCs, but Microsoft, Google and Apple hate making calendars that work with each other; Zoom, Teams and Hangouts battle away for supremacy, making joining a call more complex than before.

We no longer think about what ISP (internet service provider) to use when using the internet or how long we are using it for, but we have to think about cookies, and accept or reject them all day long.

If you travelled the world a mere 10 years ago you would think a lot about money. There would be ATMs that wouldn't accept your card, many stores and most taxis wouldn't take credit cards, you'd be doing endless maths to figure out what each note was worth, and doing all you could to spend your money before leaving a country.

Today we live in a post-electrical, post-computerized age. We don't reflect on how many hours a day we use power; we don't think of what appliances are electric, or how many have chips or motors in them. The technology revolutions in the last few hundred years have been the steam revolution, the electrical revolution and most recently the 'computing' revolution. In many ways the next revolution is the application of computers and connectivity to form the 'digital' revolution. This is an era of connected devices, abundant computing power, vast troves of data, and a degree of automation. It's a particularly fascinating revolution as many of us, myself included, have experienced life before it, in the pre-digital age.

## The pre-digital age

Remember an age where devices had just one function? You owned a TV, a radio, a CD player, each doing one thing. You had encyclopedias, a telephone book, and taxis were called AAAcars because they came first in the Yellow Pages, while others invested in easy-to-remember phone numbers.

Retail was either in-store or via mail-order home shopping, or, if you were impatient, the phone: 'Dial now, if operators are busy, do try later' and 'Please allow six to eight weeks for delivery'.

Banknotes and coins were our primary way to spend money. We had credit cards too, with the 'shunk shunk' of carbon paper, and cheque books, a sort of IOU note that people took seriously.

It may not have seemed like it at the time, but in retrospect, life was simple. Progress was steady but largely linear. Of course, things changed: we invented video cassette recorders and eventually found out how to program them; watches had thermometers added because, well, they could. Cassettes fell aside as the compact disc took over. The changes were small. They didn't change the retail landscape or logistics supply chain. They were incremental improvements, not leaps. Above all else, things just worked. There were no software updates to get headphones to work, a light switch didn't need a firmware flash, and in a world with no connectivity your toaster didn't stop talking to your kettle because it never started to.

We cared about what pictures we took because we could only take as many as the films we carried could store, and getting them printed, the only way to see what we took, was expensive and took time. It was a land of the physical. Cars were chosen on how they looked, how they handled the road, how they were made. Specifications and improvements were very tactile: a better TV was a bigger TV with a crisper picture. Better loud-speakers could go louder and be a bit more bassy. As things got older, from radios to cars to cameras, things got worn out, and worse, cassettes got mangled, CDs scratched. This was life in the analogue age.

We owned a lot of things, but we had to. While we spent a lot of our disposable income on things, it never seemed extravagant. Overlaps were small so the benefit each device brought was simple and clear.

## The mid-digital age

At first, the pre-digital age evolved slowly. Products became digitized. Photos became bits. Knowledge moved from volumes of encyclopedias to Encarta on a CD (or 20). At first the change wasn't great. While CDs were technically digital, they felt physical in nature. Renting a DVD wasn't a different behaviour to renting a VHS tape. We still lived in an era of limited choice of most things, of geography being key to retail, of distribution being a key cost.

The internet started to change things, but we still 'looked at the past in the rear-view mirror'. The phone book became an online directory. Printed magazines became websites. Newspapers became 'digital paper' versions of what we knew, and we placed the same content 'online'. It seemed little about the fundamental dynamics of the world shifted at first. We applied technology, we didn't disrupt with it.

This means we live both with the past and the future at the same time. We invent voice interfaces but keep the mouse command; we invent digital payments but keep cash and credit cards.

I call this 'peak complexity'. We are in the mid-digital age. This energy – the disruptive forces, the vast feeling of change, the acceleration of complexity, the stress of companies fighting for the profit margins of the past – is where we now lie. The complexity is found in every aspect of our lives.

Payment systems don't make sense. If you jump in any taxi in any city and ask if they take credit cards, they either scoff 'of course yes', or 'heck no'. It's a time where the teething problems of digitalization and the battles for territory define our experience.

More than anything we have the wonderful and amazing promise of the new built on the foundations of the past. Websites that at first look amazing but within four clicks lead you to an old back-end system they hoped you'd never find. Amazing mobile apps for companies, clearly designed by better teams and with more money than was available for the clunky website. Airlines that offer pilots iPads to speed up paperwork, but still need dot-matrix printouts of the manifest paperwork on blue computer paper.

What binds all these lacklustre experiences and all the perceived errors together, and what more positively shows the way into the future, is that, so far, we've translated pre-digital thinking and pulled it through a digital lens. We've taken every behaviour, product or physical item and changed it remarkably little. Everything we see today is a mere iteration of the past, incremental improvements of the old with added technology.

### We've built on the limitations of the past

It explains why online shopping appears both brand new, innovative and slick, but happens to mirror the exact same choice and design architecture from catalogues from a bygone age. We see catalogue shopping of the 1960s but with a website and email functionality. It is so exciting to think of what we can do if we dare to work around what technology can now enable. How can we rethink online shopping? What can car insurance become? How can people pay for things most easily? These are wonderful times to be in business.

## The post-digital age

*The first internet era: digitizing interfaces that already existed (catalogues newspapers). Now: creating the ones that should have existed.* LEVIE, 2014

I want you to imagine a world where everyone on the planet is given a smartphone and internet connection if they can't afford it, and training if they need it.

I want you to imagine a world now where we've never known the concept of a TV channel, or album, or banknote, or welfare cheque, or a signature, or planning permission, or resumes, or ownership, or cars, or passports, or laws, or schools, or photographs, or real-estate agents, or banks, or shopping malls, or anything we have today. It's almost impossible, but just imagine constructing the world from nothing, not around what we have. Would we have cars piling up and down roads, and also filling our residential streets, when we also have amazing electronic scooters or buses that use machine learning to serve people in the best way for everyone? Would we have offices we go to 9–5? Would we make a shopping app that asks a worker to go to a store, pick items off a shelf in a beautifully lit and air-conditioned retail outlet, that another worker has just placed on a shelf? Would we ask kids to learn the same things that were learned 100 years ago? Would we navigate 812 random TV stations to watch what we want? Would we have an internet clogged with fake traffic, bots and algorithms designed to make us outraged?

Clearly some of these things are far-fetched, but what does a world built around new technology look like?

Apple's Face ID system uses a camera to capture accurate face data by projecting and analysing over 30,000 invisible dots on your face. It automatically adapts to changes in your appearance, like wearing make-up or growing facial hair. It's pretty advanced stuff. But it's quite common in the United States to be required to both use face ID and wave your hand across a piece of paper as a proper signature. Why are the most vital documents we ever have, like car titles or passports, still physical items, sent via the mail? In fact, why are the very most secure, urgent and important things we need in life almost always only sent by mail when email offers far more security?

If everyone has a smartphone, how does that change how government assistance works? What becomes of food stamps or child nutrition programmes if people can use a phone to pay for things?

Why are newspapers funded either on the principle that you subscribe to them or that you are to be assaulted by advertising and your eyeballs monetized? How have we failed to find a way to pay for the articles that we enjoy on an individual basis?

## The post-digital age gives us a chance to rethink the world

It would be fun to consider this: what if we didn't have boarding passes as digital equivalents of paper boarding passes, but could board a plane with nothing but our face? Or we never needed to carry a credit card because our payment was linked to our face or fingerprint? This all goes to show that it's rethinking the process that's hard. What needs to change is the underlying system.

In this post-digital age, we will think about people in the age of technology, not the technology itself. We will reinvent physical retail because online behaviours mean we now expect to find things fast, see items that go alongside them and never have to queue to pay.

We will make better products that do more than the sum of their parts, like the Nest thermostat – not just the first thermostat that you can program without a computer science degree, but a thermostat that learns and makes your home more efficient, without you doing anything.

The post-digital age will be amazing. Like pre-digital, nobody will think of 'digital' in this age. The concept will move into the background and, much like oxygen or electricity, we'll understand digital to be transformative yet irrelevant. There will be no more 'chief digital officers' in the same way that a 'chief electricity officer' doesn't exist today.

In the post-digital age, digital technology will be a vast, quiet element forming the seamless backbone of life. The internet will be a background utility, noticeable only by its absence. Smart homes will work. Video will follow us around. Content will be paid for... all seamlessly and effortlessly.

We will no longer talk of TV vs online, or mobile vs desktop. Retailers won't consider online vs physical as a division worthy of note; they will just celebrate sales. Advertising will work around people, seamlessly telling sequential stories to move people to purchase. Content won't care about national boundaries; even contemporary notions like currency or language will become less central to life.

In the post-digital age, maybe we won't build libraries to access books, maybe we'll establish that we should ensure everyone has a smartphone. Maybe we'll vote securely and immediately and for virtually no cost on key issues of governance.

People will be born truly digitally native. Parents won't feel as anxious as they currently do about their children using these technologies. Kids will instinctively use them as babies, and continue to develop and nurture them as they grow alongside technology. Perhaps the most blurred line will be that between the real and the virtual. Our sense of reality, of time and place, will be the most complex for us to understand.

The post-digital age will be an entirely new landscape of behaviours and possibilities and in order to best understand how to grow and prosper in this wild new horizon, we need to understand how ideas develop, improve and fit together, and to do this we need to understand the idea of the paradigm shift.

### ACTION

Channel your inner eight-year-old, find any core industry or process and very incessantly and naïvely ask 'why' and 'how' a few times. Why do we have a legal drinking age? How do you prove it? Why is it this way? But why? But why?

Maybe it's the home buying process, or the way benefits are paid, or any part of the healthcare process or the military. Do so with an eye for the fundamental shifts in what technology makes possible. Which again, given most eight-year-olds, is not much of a leap of faith. If you have an eight-year-old to hand, even better. Maybe ask them to create a new mindset or approach to any key industry. Or go one step further and just get them to build a scope of work like a consultancy, pay them a handsome retainer and take their 67-slide deck to a CEO or politician near you and invoice them.

## CHAPTER THREE

# Disruption and the paradigm shift

*The best swordsman in the world doesn't need to fear the
second-best swordsman in the world; no, the person for him to
be afraid of is some ignorant antagonist who has never had a
sword in his hand before; he doesn't do the thing he ought to
do, and so the expert isn't prepared for him.* MARK TWAIN

It's fascinating that a quote that best explains how the spirit of
disruption doesn't come from a startup founder at last year's
TechCrunch or from a venture capital expert in Silicon Valley
but from a writer, more than 120 years ago, about medieval
conflict. It sometimes seems that leading businesses are ignorant
and antagonistic.

When the iPhone launched in 2007, it was both the best
phone the world had ever seen and Apple's first-ever phone.
Dyson's first vacuum cleaner was the best vacuum ever made at
launch. When Tony Fadell made Nest Lab's first thermostat, it
was clearly the world's best.

From Tesla's first-ever car setting the standard for the entire
car industry, to Uber's first taxi business, to Amazon's first

attempt at retail, it seems that the real step changes in how things are done come from those who've never done it before. Facebook is by far the biggest, most profitable media owner the world has ever seen, led by a CEO who never worked a day in his life in a media company. Donald Trump's first-ever role in politics was being the leader of the free world: he broke all the rules, he didn't let knowing nothing whatsoever about government or politics or how politicians were supposed to behave get in the way. Far from it, and it raises a great question. Have these companies or people succeeded in changing the game despite a lack of experience, or because of it?

Why is SpaceX doing things that are way beyond what NASA with its long history could do? Why did Sonos make connected speakers before Sony or Bose? Why didn't a train company invent the Hyperloop? Why didn't a helicopter company rather than a Chinese toy maker invent the first drone that can carry a person? Why didn't a bank or a mobile operator that owns the financial relationship with customers invent Apple Pay? Why did it take Amazon to invent the Echo speaker when Apple had Siri years earlier? If Instagram is about sharing Kodak moments, why didn't Kodak come up with it?

*If Instagram is about sharing Kodak moments, why didn't Kodak come up with it?*

It's easy to think this is survivorship bias, that only the winners get to write history, that luck played a vital role. So, in this chapter we're going to look at how this has happened. What have these companies done that is so remarkable? Why is expertise seemingly unhelpful? What does disruption mean? Most usefully of all, what can my company do about it today?

## A new theory for disruption

When we talk of disruption these days, we naturally think back to Clayton Christensen's globally renowned idea that disruption is about companies which undermine legacy players based on a new technology at a lower price point.

It's based on the idea that companies are disrupted because of their success, that they are so invested in a wonderfully profitable way to extract the most money from a product, and doing it so well, that they never seek to explore ways to do things differently. It is because of this happy complacency that they become vulnerable.

Then another company, using a new form of technology, enters what appears to be a different market, at a much lower price point. The new entrant suddenly or slowly expands in quality or role, to undermine the incumbent's success.

We can see how, for example, *Encyclopædia Britannica's* expensive yet wonderful leather books were rapidly undermined by Wikipedia's web-based and communally resourced product. We can see how Kodak made a bucket-load of cash in the making of film and its processing, and that while they recognized the significance of digital photography, it wasn't a can of worms they wanted to open.

Now the spirit of this idea – another company with different expertise and a different way of looking at things – is a key concept, but the idea that the disruption happens from below is massively misleading. I think the idea that disruptors offer initially inferior but cheaper products is absolutely wrong.

## ACTION

I don't mind how you do it, but come up with a list of 10 new companies or products or brands that seem successful, heralded and new age.

And try to consider if they are really following the theory of disruption or something else. If something else, what is it that they do remarkably? A great idea, a great brand, a great premium product etc.

Uber was never a cheaper way to hail a taxi; it was originally a more convenient way to get a far nicer, more expensive method of transport. Tesla's cars are by no means cheaper to buy or make, but they are changing the entire automotive industry because they have altered everything from how cars are designed and made, to how they are sold and repaired. They are slowly changing the industry, not by being cheaper or undermining incumbents in a few ways but by reimagining every element in the sector.

While Airbnb may be altering many aspects of the hotel industry – and being 'disruptive', the product is vastly different – it's for people who want to stay somewhere bigger, more personal, who want to have a genuine experience. In many cases people spend more money on their stay in an Airbnb than they would have on a hotel.

From Netflix to Facebook to Amazon to Alibaba and most of the world in which we live, the new companies that have developed have largely not been cheaper, but better. They have created better customer experiences, offered faster delivery, allowed people to do more, helped people get what they wanted. Clayton Christensen's theory does not explain how Nest became a $3.2 billion company making a far more expensive thermostat, or how Dyson was able to charge more than three times the average selling price of vacuums in 2002 and still capture a huge part of the market.

It appears that 'disruption' was a theory based on selected data from a narrow window of time, in a linear world of manufacturing physical products, with examples from the world of data storage technology and excavator design around 40 years ago.

It's damaging to think of technology in that way. To base business thinking on Clayton Christensen's theory limits companies' desire and ability to see and drive more exciting opportunities. It is far more empowering, exciting and profitable to focus on what technology can now allow us to make or what consumers really dream of having. In particular the money to be made by makings things easier or simpler is clear to see.

It is much better to focus on doing extra and more, than to be paranoid about companies undercutting you and being cheaper. We need the spirit of disruption to be about optimism and creation, not paranoia and defence. Disruption is a rampantly overused word. It's become filler for press releases, standard-issue wording for insane videos about the future and base material for PowerPoint slides.

## The power of the paradigm shift

Toyota employed some of the best electrical engineers in the world to tell it that the things Tesla were secretly working on were impossible. This perhaps best explains Tesla, which with less than 15 years' experience in the car industry, can make vehicles that accelerate faster than any other road car ever known. Who on earth is Elon Musk to come into this category and do what is widely thought to be impossible?

How can the Tesla Model S Plaid be so much faster than a Lamborghini Huracán, Bugatti Chiron or a McLaren 720S, while costing typically 10 times less and despite their competitors having 10 times more experience making cars?

How can they make a car that gets better as it ages, improving overnight thanks to software updates? The Tesla Model S looks radically different from cars that are far slower, it carries five adults, and it's not low to the ground. How can it sell a $10,000 upgrade that is software and thus has zero marginal cost and thus at 100 per cent margin? This is a car that breaks virtually all the category rules that have been formed and learned for decades. This chapter explores a totally new way to think about progress and business disruption and creates a new theory for it.

It was Thomas Kuhn, the US physicist, historian and philosopher of science, who wrote a book in 1962 called *The Structure of Scientific Revolutions* and in it coined the term 'paradigm shift' (Kuhn, 1962).

Kuhn's book focuses on the way that scientific knowledge progresses. It discusses the idea that the world comes together and gets aligned in one particular way of seeing the world that becomes fixed. Typically, there is a system of beliefs or viewpoints or universal truths that enable people to make sense of the world. At any one time, these beliefs are based on assumptions that the majority of people are happy to regard as being fixed.

This viewpoint and mental framework form the basis of other experiments and procedures, and ideally these will continue to build confidence in this viewpoint or paradigm. We are generally sure today that atoms exist, that the earth is not flat and rotates around the sun; in fact almost all scientific principles are created and aligned in reference to each other. By being sure of the speed of light, we can calculate the size of the solar system; with Einstein's mass-energy equivalence we can develop GPS navigation or the atomic bomb.

Yet sometimes, a breakthrough is made that challenges everything we previously thought. At this point it's clear that everything we think was known, every characteristic or variable we fixed, may no longer be the case. It's this huge shift from one way of seeing things to another that has been coined the 'paradigm shift'.

Obsolete or superseded theories are common in science. We had phlogistic chemistry as a theory until the 1770s, and the caloric theory of thermodynamics explained much of the world until the mid-1800s when it was thought heat consisted of a self-repellent fluid called caloric that flowed from hotter bodies to colder bodies.

The danger of a paradigm is that we seek to make sense of it more than we seek to destroy it, because so much rests upon it. Paradigms are based on a system of thinking that all makes sense together; we fix some variables and create linkages with other variables and before we know where we are we have an entire system that seems to make sense. In a much more mundane sense, our lives consist of these very interconnected systems. Living in a world where we went to the office from 9 to 5, Monday to Friday, our lives became fixed around that. We'd do grocery shopping on the way home from work because it seemed more sensible than having delivery drivers drop off goods to empty households while we were away. We'd pick up kids from after-school gymnastics and use the time before to sneak into a shopping centre. Coffee shops in city centres swelled with weary train commuters, weekends were sacred; it certainly wasn't the optimal way to live life, but it was one that made sense within the boundaries that we had created and stuck to. When the pandemic forced everybody to stay at home, we suddenly jumped to a new paradigm. There was nothing to stop grocery deliveries arriving seamlessly into our apartments, and Zoom calls became the rigid cadence to life where being late or not turning up became inexcusable. In this context, trips to department stores or to coffee shops seem to make little sense. Our cities have built up this way around our habits: newsagents and coffee near London Underground stations, sandwich shops around lunch breaks in city centres. We made spaces and time around the shared universal criterion of the working pattern of the late 20th century. That is apart from doctors, dentists, hairdressers, car repair places, solicitors and, well, a crazy number of entities that all wanted to work standard hours and ignore when many people had free time, but that's another matter.

The modern world before the 2020 Covid-19 pandemic made sense and the switch to a post-pandemic world is hard; it becomes a hybrid life between the paradigms of remote and office work. There is superstition and jealousy for those who appear to do well from working in an office. In a world where most meetings are face to face, video calls soon lose appeal because taking them from the back of a taxi on the way to a meeting is rather difficult.

Kuhn's theory of paradigms is generally only ever applied to scientific beliefs, or ways of seeing the world, but there is merit in the idea of tensions between groups of people who, at the time, fix assumptions, before someone smashes them and huge progress is made. I want to apply this type of mechanic to how creativity and design progress. I want to explain how disruption in business is the leap to a new paradigm, much like Kuhn's theory.

## Design as evolutionary funnels

If you ask a person to draw anything on any medium with any implement, they freeze. If you ask a graphic designer to design a logo and give them nothing to work on, they can't do anything. An architect with no brief or budget, a creative in an ad agency with no problem to solve, it's all the same. Design needs constraints. All design must be shaped by elements.

Yet if you ask a group of people casually to draw a house, most people will draw something remarkably childlike and remarkably similar. We have inherently fixed in our heads an idea of what a house must be, how it is drawn, how big it will be on the paper, what viewpoint it should come from. This preconceived idea of what a home should look like is based on how we think things should be done and how things have been done before.

We make many more assumptions than we realize when we design. They may be based on things we invented, things we remember from the past, groupthink, or many other unnecessarily fixed criteria. This is natural. In a massively complex world we have to fight to make sense of, we can't continually challenge everything. We don't wake up in the morning unsure if we should accept that gravity exists, or that up isn't down; it would be exhausting. Nor can you be open to everything. If you're designing a new sofa, you can't be an expert in leather tanning and ergonomics, and then also ponder the implications for your design of new developments in graphene (an incredibly flexible substance 200 times stronger than steel, which is currently impossible to use).

As a result, any design process follows an iterative process based on a certain set of assumptions. These become spoken or unspoken design parameters.

Normally we start with a goal or problem or brief; we then start to explore options based on design criteria; and slowly, over time, collectively or individually, we improve and refine the design. Often this process isn't smooth; often progress grinds to a halt, or reaches a dead end. Generally speaking, progress towards ever better solutions starts fast, with huge initial improvements. Then slowly, the process hits what we commonly refer to as the law of diminishing returns, whereby improvements produce relatively smaller increases in output.

A key part of this process is that, as the technology matures, it tends to converge on relatively similar optimum solutions, as illustrated in Figure 3.1. Websites today look more similar to each other than when people first started designing them; hotel rooms today now look broadly alike because lessons have been shared; mobile phones once looked radically different, now they look the same.

FIGURE 3.1 A brief to the optimal solution

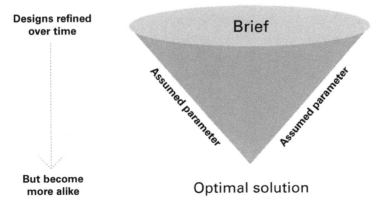

FIGURE 3.2  A brief to the new optimal solution

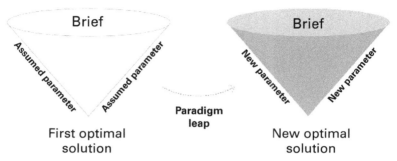

Design is evolution – through error or hypothesis or fresh thinking, we slowly mutate and adapt in different ways, before we generally become more similar.

Eventually, just as everything has converted to one optimal solution that everybody adopts, finds agreeable, and is likely most commercially successful, a paradigm leap can be made whereby the assumed parameters can change to new parameters, and a new quest towards the new optimal solution can begin, as illustrated in Figure 3.2.

When we celebrate the Nest thermostats, the Ubers of the world, the iPhones, Dysons and Blackberries, we really celebrate those who unleash the power of the paradigm shift. They leap from one world of possibilities to another, they challenge the parameters used by everyone else to shape their designs and solutions. They leap from one paradigm to another, to an optimal solution based on a whole new world of thinking. This is a paradigm leap, and it's the essence of disruption.

## The paradigm leap in action

On 1 July 1979, the first Sony Walkman went on sale, launching a new era in music (Haire, 2009). Sony had just created the first-ever personal music player. We could now take the music we loved with us, and without the arm-ache of the ghetto blaster. It came at a cost. The first personal cassette players were massive, cost the equivalent of $500 at today's currency exchange rates, had terrible sound quality, skipped badly, offered awful battery life, and best (or worst!) of all, didn't even have a rewind function. We had to spin tapes around on pencils. It's wonderful to look back at our consumption of albums on tape and the thinking we did. The product was a reasonable success, selling out 30,000 units in the first three months in Japan (Adner, 2012).

Over a period of decades, with huge R&D investments from Sony and competitors alike, many errors, as well as endless rounds of customer feedback, things got much, much better. Not least the name. First marketed in the United States as the Soundabout, it was soon changed to the Walkman, and came in a choice of colours. Despite the competition, Sony kept ahead of its rivals. Even 10 years after its first device, Sony's Walkman retained a 50 per cent market share in the United States and 46 per cent in Japan, in a space seething with competitors. Sony maintained its profit margin, regardless of the entry of many new competitors to the market, with a price premium of approximately $20 over rival offers (Adner, 2012).

Over time the device improved. It got Dolby (B, then C), rechargeable batteries, even rewind buttons. Engineers got better at making components smaller, as they always do, so the size of the personal cassette player got smaller, until finally, with a smart aluminium casing, it was only a little bigger than the cassette itself. Miniaturization wasn't easy; batteries needed to be improved, motors needed to get more efficient, step-up converters were invented and made smaller. At the same time the device got way cheaper. By 2002 it wasn't uncommon to see personal radio cassette players in gas stations for those impulse purchases on the go. Designers had fun; we got sports models with yellow plastic, radio functions were added. Life was good.

The improvements came fast then slowed down, and it got to a point where the improvements got smaller. It was easy to reduce the size initially but once it had shrunk to barely bigger than a cassette tape, improvements were marginal, and the law of diminishing returns set in.

## The CD player era

At the time the Walkman design peaked – the very best music-playing machine the world had ever collectively crafted – came the very worst personal CD player ever made. It was huge, far more expensive than the best Walkman it replaced at $450, and had an awful battery life. It would skip all the time. The LCD was tiny and displayed very little information. It was the worst CD player ever, but it was still better than the best Walkman. This was digital sound. It came with no tape degradation and no winding in the spaghetti after an accident.

We'd made a paradigm leap. We'd gone from ever smaller, incremental design improvements that worked towards an increasingly easy-to-envision optimal goal, with everyone on the same page and working towards solving the same problems, to a whole new canvas for design where the end result wasn't clear.

We now had new criteria against which to optimize design, new constraints to shape the progress towards the optimal design and new problems to solve. The criteria that once held back the cassette player were different. The problems to solve now were new and the expertise needed wildly different. Laser engineers replaced electromagnetic sensor experts and Dolby engineers were replaced by people who knew about caching digital memory to stop skipping. Designers who loved slow, high-torque motors now needed to know about fast-spinning, low-torque designs.

Even recording music faced new challenges. How do you compress music without making it seem cold and flat? Can you remove information about frequencies we can't hear without changing the soul of the music? Even breaking up music from continuous to segmented had rather profound meanings: for example, is it okay to have 'tracks' of a few seconds between other tracks or should those little warm-up flurries or contextual introductions be attached to the song?

## The worst MP3 players

As Discmans became marvellously cheap, remarkably thin, and music moved from analogue to digital, someone had a new idea: what if the physical media wasn't needed? What if the music was lifted and liberated from the storage medium and was stored in the music player? This was a huge shift. Until now music had been physical, and media had been too. We lived with VHS tapes, magazines, CDs, laser disks. Media was something we bought and touched. Facing high costs of storage, music could only be digitized if it was compressed, and the MP3 format was born.

The first-ever MP3 player was of course both marvellous and awful. It was launched in 1997 by SaeHan Information Systems, and sold as its 'MPMan' player in Asia in the spring of 1998 (Van Buskirk, 2005). While the battery power was fine, the device small and not too expensive, new issues arose. User experience was a concern. To put music into the device, the music first had to be encoded in the MP3 format by an encoder provided by the user, and then transferred via the parallel port to the docking station that connected to the portable player device. Another issue was storage: the two versions of the player offered 32 or 64MBs of capacity, enough to store a measly 6 or 12 songs, less than most albums.

There were legal issues too. MP3 files were not readily available. The Recording Industry Association of America (RIAA) Associate Director of Anti-Copyright Infringement, Frank Creighton, initially said the MPMan had 'no function other than playing material that was stolen from record companies' (Kaufman, 1998).

It's here we first see the uncomfortable relationship between regulation and the law and the spirit of disruption, a topic we will visit later in this book.

The problems the MP3 player brought with it were again totally new. The company that would produce a breakthrough wouldn't be Sony, with their amazing engineers who'd perfected CDs and lasers and cassettes and motors. It wouldn't be a company that knew batteries better than anyone. It wouldn't be material scientists who could make things thinner. It would be people who understood the human-centred design experience. People who knew that in this era, how the product functioned was not the most vital thing. It would be companies that understood software and that were also large enough to negotiate with the record industry and be taken seriously. It was of course unlikely to be a company like Sony, which was making too much money selling physical music.

What made the iPod successful wasn't the iPod. It was iTunes, and it took time. Steve Jobs knew that on its own the MP3 player was useless. He knew that in order for the device to have value, other building blocks needed to be in place first. The success of the iPod would be dependent not on a better device but on a better ecosystem: a faster internet to make downloading songs fast enough, record labels to be ready to sell music as MP3 files. He realized that innovation was never about being first per se, but being first in a meaningful way at the right time.

The first-generation iPod for Mac retailed at $399 and could store up to 1,000 songs. It was a revelation. Now you could take any piece of music you could ever hope to own with you. It had an intuitive interface design and was lightweight. Despite being available only for Mac users, which was 10 per cent of all computer users at the time, the iPod was the fastest-selling MP3 player to ever hit the market (Adner, 2012).

We had entered the paradigm where software mattered more than hardware. Apple announced the iTunes Music Store, an online retail hub to browse and purchase music for 99 cents per song, and within two years iTunes' library had grown to 1.5 million songs. Apple had understood the relationship between service and device. It would make little profit from selling songs at 99 cents per download, but the ecosystem mattered. The iTunes store gave the iPod legitimacy in a world of shady MP3 accessibility.

MP3 players got better, but not quite in the same way. They got smaller and lighter, storage was increased, devices were cheaper, but progress felt different. It was more about the interface. Apple iTunes was most people's main experience of the device. It became about how easy it was to find music, how nice it felt to do so. It became about reducing the pain points of coding music in such a way that it aided distribution, or digital rights management protection. It was about making payment easy, making synchronizing seem obvious. More than anything else, Apple had to guide people into a new way of thinking about music in the easiest way possible. Again, the skills needed were different and put the focus on coders, not engineers, as well as user interface design, not product design. Deals had to be made with record labels rather than with aluminium rollers. Most core Apple staff skills were more useful in this paradigm.

Our relationship with technology changed too. We expected to own more, to listen to what we wanted when we wanted. We'd skip things we didn't love or feel like at that time. Technology started to shape how we behaved now, not reflect how we behaved then.

iPods took over the world, music became digital, and the development of the internet and the shift to the smartphone brought another huge paradigm shift.

## The streaming age

The internet meant we no longer needed to own music, we just needed access to it. As home broadband became more prevalent and 3G connectivity spread on phones, we no longer needed to store music or to own music; we just needed to access it, at all times, immediately.

And this is where we are now. The world of portable music blends into the world of smartphone design. We now find ourselves with faster connectivity, better battery life, a need for music videos, for higher-resolution screens, for larger OLED screens. The whole paradigm has shifted again.

Phones have changed so much of our lives and so many industries. Even in the specific context of music, they changed more than we ever realized, and they once again changed our relationship with music. Walkmans allowed us to take music with us, to augment our lives; CDs allowed us to listen only to the music we loved, letting us skip tracks immediately; MP3 players allowed us to think of music with abundance, not scarcity; and streaming meant we discovered and selected music in new ways.

Streaming means the new challenges are of managing abundance, aiding discovery, and making money in this era. Our relationship moved from the album to the single, from the record label to the content gateway. The distribution costs of music, the hosting and the production, tended to zero.

We no longer needed record labels to make well-produced music and distribute it. We no longer need companies to merchandise it, nor albums bundled as units to 'buy' and to access music. We care about Spotify or Apple Music or Pandora; we don't care about physical media, record labels, bitrates, and costs.

---

Perhaps fun isn't the word, but it's interesting to think of other paradigms. We have paradigms in public transportation, paradigms in personal technology, in the transportation of goods. Planes went from being propellor to jet propelled; we had steam-driven trains, then diesel, then electric and perhaps one day the hyperloop. Have a think about the various paradigms of design. Which of these seem to be ending?

## Leaps in design paradigms surround us

The changes in music devices follow a set pattern: technology and design make radical progress, which then slows to find an optimal device, followed by a huge leap to another way of thinking. This is not something unique to personal music. We see these leaps everywhere.

When transporting goods in the UK, for example, for millennia we functioned with the paradigm of transporting goods by horse, before a sudden move to shipping goods by canal resulted in increased construction of canals. These canals improved in their setup and construction over time, to be replaced dramatically by the advent of a cheaper and faster method of transporting goods: railway. Railway technology in turn progressed in huge leaps and bounds before being destroyed again by the use of large trucks transporting goods via roads.

With personal transportation we've had the era of horseback riding, then horse-drawn cars, then combustion-powered horseless carriages, and now it looks as if we're on the edge of the next paradigm, electric-powered cars. In the future cars may become entirely self-driving, and this technology may be expensive, but if cars can move without us, why would we park them, blocking up space and rendering them underutilized? So, it seems likely that self-driving cars won't be owned, but accessed. We may go from the era of owning, maintaining and loving cars to the era of getting access to self-driving cars. Suddenly car parking spaces are entirely freed up as cars can move around freely and out of cities when demand is lower. Suddenly our commutes may become longer and more productive and the shape and size of cities may change.

Cars themselves will change. Vehicles are currently designed to be suitable for all the most common types of usage. A typical adult needs a car that fits five people, can travel at 85 mph and can do 400-mile journeys with ease, even if they drive it alone 95 per cent of the time, at less than 40 mph and do fewer than 40 miles per day. If we are to access self-driving cars there is no reason why they shouldn't be much more specialized vehicles. We may have lounge-like vehicles stacked with large screens and room for eight people for multi-family trips. We may see absurd luxury cars that fit two people for couples' romantic weekends, or pod-like vehicles that fit one person and no luggage, travel at less than 50 mph and act only for commuters. More will change in this paradigm than anyone realizes.

We have had eras of shopping: the local store, the department store, the shopping mall and now online stores. Paradigms are everywhere. We once kept time with sundials, then had large mechanical clocks in town centres, then mechanical pocket watches, quartz watches, and now two-thirds of teenagers don't carry a watch at all, they use their phone (Clark, 2007). Increasingly what we wear on our wrists is either a luxury watch as a sign of status, or something more about monitoring our health or making payments than telling the time.

The phone has eaten other devices too. We had the paradigm of the camera obscura, then the photographic camera, the digital camera, and now we just tend to use phones. Initially, smartphones increased demand for proper cameras, before becoming so good that they ate that market. We had black and white cathode ray tubes in televisions once, then the colour CRT TV, then we saw plasma TVs develop, to be overtaken by LCD and then LED TVs. Yet now increasingly we watch videos on our phones and not on the television.

The world of currency and money has had similar shifts: we had the era of cowrie shells and other forms of items of rareness, then we shifted and coins developed, and we had units of money with an intrinsic value. We then leapt to the idea of banknotes, the concept of the promissory note where something had no inherent value but was deemed by all to be trusted. We then shifted to another paradigm with the first credit cards, where the entire transaction was unattached to the physical token (a credit card isn't a note, it's a shortcut to a digital transaction). Now we tend to use physical currency less and less, we use formal bank and credit card transactions less, we use apps like Venmo or WeChat Pay or Alipay.

And the very foundations of currency and money could be radically altered by digital thinking. For 5,000 years, gold's combination of scarcity, lustre, malleability and density made it uniformly desirable and a perfect global utility to tie money to. But after 1931 in the UK and the US in 1933, every nation on earth moved to a 'fiat' system, coming from the Latin word 'fieri', meaning by decree. This is a monetary system in which the value of currency is allowed to fluctuate dynamically against other currencies on the foreign exchange markets. Here the value of money is determined by a government, the health of their economy and monetary policy. Digital currency in the form of cryptocurrency is an entirely inverted philosophy where value is linked to scarcity, where value is uniform globally and where there are no centralized systems to alter value; a digital currency's value is set by the market, and is thus in theory decentralized. There is a theory that if coins and notes are pre-digital money, and credit cards and digital wallets are interim mid-digital-age solutions, a form of crypto would be philosophically a post-digital money system, the one we'd design from scratch if we made the world now.

It seems almost clichéd to talk about Tesla as a disruptive startup. I'm keen to write a book that is fresh and shines new light onto new topics, so to be one of many people celebrating the thinking of Tesla feels a little bit uncomfortable. But a few things are worth sharing.

There are two ways to make an electric car. One is to start with a conventional car, remove the engine and drive train, add in a battery, a bit of new software and hope to figure it out. Such vehicles don't come close to leveraging the benefits of electrically propelled vehicles (EVs).

Designing an EV platform from scratch changes everything. For one, the chassis can be much lighter since structural points are designed specifically for a battery pack in the floor and light electric motors at each axle. An EV allows for totally different shapes of vehicle. Car designers are conventionally restrained by the need to fit in a vast powertrain, a bulky engine, a variety of moving parts, which must be readily accessed. An EV can almost be any shape; the battery can be placed low to the ground, giving better performance and a lower centre of gravity but also better interior space and more cargo space.

By building from scratch, Tesla was able to rethink every single electrical component; they designed a car that could be upgraded by software, a vehicle with an entirely new computer system.

At the same time, Tesla requires very different workers to solve very different problems. The benefit of being a new car company is it doesn't have a legacy of car dealerships, but it means Tesla needs an army of lawyers to help battle lawmakers who insist on them, so it now needs to design cars that require less maintenance to ensure this strategy makes sense. But by far the greatest problem facing Tesla is the need to build out a charging network; it's more like a mobile operator building out a network than a car maker.

## What is disruption?

Having been rather rude about Clayton Christensen's definition of disruption, I do offer my own approach:

> The process of challenging widely held assumptions to create a significant business advantage that comes from an understanding of consumers' needs.

Challenging widely held assumptions is how Red Bull can make a disgusting drink that can create an entire new drinks category, or how L'eggs, a brand of women's tights back in 1969 from Hanes, dominated the market by being placed in grocery stores packaged in plastic eggs. It explains how Ryanair can fill flights to city pairs that nobody thought anyone would want to fly between.

The business advantage may come from reducing costs to make, distribute, market or service items, something closer to Clayton's original theory, but it can also come from increasing revenue by selling to more people or more often, or having the ability to charge more, or by selling something in addition. This may be by creating a new market, or eating into an existing one.

An element of the thinking behind a car-sharing app like Turo, or home-sharing service like Airbnb, or music streaming app like Spotify, is that the cost of providing a car, or room, or music is cheaper than owning and maintaining cars or hotels, or making and distributing records. Direct-to-consumer startups are often (but not always) rooted in the idea that they can sell things that were already being bought by people, and use more efficient marketing with better data, in a way where they cut out the middleman and therefore increase the margin they make.

Nespresso thinks they can not only get us to buy coffee in a more expensive way, but do so more regularly, and create a new market in between expensive takeaway coffee from Starbucks and cheap home-brewed coffee.

Many companies are disruptive in many ways. Tesla not only wants to eat into the existing market share for sedans, but also to create new revenue streams by selling $10,000 software to make cars drive themselves a bit more, while also cutting out the cost of a dealership network, while also selling emissions credits and selling electricity at charging points, while also creating a brand and PR approach so admired that it saves on the cost of advertising.

Tesla in 2021 has company books that look like no other; it made $101 million betting on Bitcoin, $518 million on emissions credits, and spent $0 on sales and marketing (Ramey, 2021).

Not all transformative leaps are rooted in technology. When Innocent Smoothies 'disrupted' sales of soft drinks and captured incredible market share and a leapfrog in profit per drink sold, it was down to a nice new idea, great packaging and crushing fruit, not some tech gadgetry. When mattress brand Casper challenged the idea that we would only ever buy a mattress after testing it instore, they sold \$1.8 million worth of mattresses in the first two months by tapping into a slightly different way to package products and hoping that consumers would take a little leap of faith (Rodic, 2017). The relationship between technology and disruption is very clear but that doesn't mean the disruption is digital transformation. In many ways what we see is more of a shift to making new, sometimes innovative things that better serve customers.

What these companies show is the focus on consumers' lives and offering them something better. Curved TVs, or 3D TVs, or smart refrigerators that have cameras inside, or the Facebook Portal family connector, or Google Glass all failed because they seemed rooted in a poor understanding of the realities of being a human. We don't want to put technology on our face yet, and likely never will en masse.

It is cheaper and more effective batteries that allow Juul to take on the tobacco industry and create a category called vaping, but it's understanding that people want this which makes it work. Greater capacity batteries and more efficient motors allowed drones to become every day, and to take on the firework business for aerial displays, which are so mesmerizing people will flock to them. Sonder, a digital-first serviced apartment rental firm, only makes sense if it can use connected smart locks and piggy-back off Airbnb's audience, but also because people like the idea of a seamless, fast check-in 24 hours a day.

And it's this focus and a deep and close sense of people and what they need that is the defining characteristic of how industry and production are changing. A time where imagination, ideas and innovation are more important than ever, but only when there is a focus on the real needs of people. Where making what people want is more crucial than making people want things, something we meet in the next chapter.

## CHAPTER FOUR

# The third era of management

*We have for many decades been living in a 'post-industrial' society. I believe we are now on the verge of a 'post-managerial' society, perhaps even a 'post-organizational' society.*

GARY HAMEL

There is a much-embraced theory that we live in the fourth industrial age. First came steam and water power to create the first era, then came electricity to transform how we made things for the second, then computerization for the third several decades ago, and we now lie on the cusp of the fourth industrial revolution. This is Industry 4.0 where we use AI and robots, and robots that make robots, and the Internet of Things, and the Internet of Systems to Make Things.

This is indeed true, but another more interesting theory is based on eras of production and management: what skills, tools and qualities have been adopted in each of these ages, what elements of the customer landscape have changed. By considering this we can see, in addition to four industrial ages, three ages of management and production.

## Moving from needs to wants

Of all the things you've bought in the last year, how many of them were bought because of needs vs wants? You may feel you needed a new pair of jeans but did you really have no other bottoms to wear? You may have felt the need for a new convertible but did you already have a way to drive around? We forget how much production and consumption patterns have shifted.

Imagine the era where the car was invented and commercialized, where the TV or radio was first introduced for sale, where you bought an array of things from electric kettles to toasters to dishwashers for the very first time. Entirely new, exciting products, that perhaps you genuinely couldn't afford at a time with little credit, these needed no selling. Things are different now; few people pine for things they NEED. For the majority of people in the world (and yes it seems distasteful at a time of great inequality and poverty to say this) the problem now is less of scarcity and more of abundance. Many people buy things because they are better, not because they are essential; they buy things to show others who they are, not to survive. Generally, we see incremental improvements in the products that we buy from year to year, as anyone with an iPhone will testify, not leaps of change that drag us to stores out of sheer delight or need.

The world of business seems to have generally pivoted from being about pushing out worthwhile products to creating demand for slightly improved versions or niche products to fill ever-smaller gaps.

We've seen so far two eras of management and production since the industrial revolution, each with two distinct mindsets guiding companies and industries, shaping how they make things, what they make, and what talent, assets, workflows and methodologies are best suited.

## Pre-management business

While the concept of organized labour has been around for thousands of years, it was generally found in areas like the military, government, perhaps a few educational establishments and the Church. Even through the Middle Ages, most entities would be small-scale, disorganized and decentralized. The owner of a farm or construction company could handle individually all of its planning, coordination, recruitment, resource allocation and sales strategy. Most entities were small businesses producing products with varying degrees of quality, low rates of productivity, and little need for managerial control beyond that of the owner or master artisan. Products were made by a single person or small group, often for specific people and their needs, with a batch size of one. Since products made by hand didn't scale very well, there was little advantage to larger orders or making larger batches. It was a period of expensively produced items that few could afford.

## Era one – a focus on execution and scale

From the late 1700s and due to the Industrial Revolution, massive changes in the way people lived and worked took place. Before this time, most people resided in rural communities, eking out a living.

The industrial revolution changed almost everything about society and business. With new technology, new products were invented and new fabrication and production techniques were created. From textiles to iron to pottery, it became clear that scale would be the ultimate advantage, and owning (and thus managing) assets became a vital way to ensure growth and profitability, as did increasing staff numbers.

In order to best deploy and coordinate labour, company structures were developed along the lines of the military to ensure clear command and control lines existed, and that there was a clear system of orchestration and a track record of events and outputs. Organizations gained scale. To coordinate these larger organizations, owners unable to order about and monitor hundreds of people needed to depend on others, and thus the concept of managers was introduced, perhaps along with jokes about middle management. By the early 1900s, the term 'management' was in wide use for the first time in business. Companies could be envisaged as machines, with people effectively becoming cogs in them. What was needed was replaceable, reliable, identical people. There was no space for thinking or training, but instead people focused on repetition.

This era was dependent on execution. And in order to best ensure this, a range of solutions and techniques were developed. This saw the advent of the specialization of labour, standardized processes, workflow planning, and the birth of quality control. For the first time we had a need to keep records, to have basic accounting and 'bookkeeping'. A climate of standardization saw the invention of the idea of bureaucracy and with it a focus on procedural regularity, a hierarchical system of accountability, and more than anything else, rigid rules and the nightmare aversion to rule breaking. Bureaucracy, which is such a staple of modern life and frustrations, is a remarkably relatively new idea, the term only coined in the mid-18th century by the French philosopher Vincent de Gournay (Starbuck, 2005).

Business management in this era was relatively simple. Scale was the ultimate goal, with first-to-market leaders creating unassailable leads that often led to near monopolies. Business and trade were largely domestic. Scale and efficiency became a feedback loop, market dominance created significant income, which could be invested to ensure further dominance, and new entrants and challengers to markets were limited by capital demands, with a lending ecosystem far from today's buoyant and rather enthusiastic venture capital or private equity markets.

The world effectively became a landgrab, making things the world needed for the first time. The key strategies for growth remained a simple list of chasing efficiency, consistency of production, and predictability of outputs.

In this period technology largely acted as a lever to our bodies, not our minds. Rather like the plough, factories allowed our muscles to accomplish more. At this time, productivity largely followed linear rules: five times more people would accomplish five times more work. People working twice as long could perhaps produce twice as many items, worth double the amount. Management wasn't rocket science, it was record keeping and something closer to whipping people than brand purpose workshops or discussions on work–life balance.

## Era two – a focus on expertise and specialization

As businesses matured and marketplaces evolved, new consumer needs followed. The world was saturated with houses connected to electricity, now needing lightbulbs and light sockets, cars needed tyres, gardens needed lawnmowers, radios needed loudspeakers. The range of products made possible by other products before them, and advances in material sciences like Bakelite, combined with labour-saving devices that allowed women to enter the workforce, increased wealth like never before. Rampant demand for products in all directions created even more opportunities for business. New market gaps allowed smaller companies to compete with large, dominant ones.

Companies began to learn more and, with effective recording, gather more and more data on potential gaps in the market, and perhaps even consumer needs. Records on what production techniques and management principles worked slowly evolved and became documented and shared. Over time the need for executional excellence became overshadowed by the benefits of expertise.

In 1911, Taylor's *Principles of Scientific Management* was published, which first raised questions of tension between the 'things of production' and the 'humanity of production', or in other words the 'numbers people' (people who looked after what was made) and the 'people people' (the people who made them) (Taylor, 1911).

As the world became ever wealthier, consumerism more rampant, and as some industries started to cannibalize, differentiation became more important. More sophisticated products and services could be produced, requiring more advanced skills and labour, and it became apparent that the endless search for scale would have limits.

Management shifted, empowered by statistical and mathematical insights, and as academics began to study management as a science, powerful new theories like management by objectives, Six Sigma and, later still, waterfall and then agile thinking for software design were developed. At the same time, organizations became more complex, demanding improved communications, especially when offices began to collaborate over large distances. The world became more globalized. The organization was still a machine, but it was sophisticated, interlinked, organic. The main driver of growth became quality, not scale; we moved from efficiency to adding value, from reducing variation and lowering errors to constant improvement. Predictable gains became a greater management goal than consistency of production. And with it grew a whole slew of management techniques, from monitoring more and more key performance indicators, to real-time reporting, to just-in-time (JIT) inventory systems. In this period, humanity was still largely about compliance. Instructions were still largely top down, and it was rarely about wild leaps of imagination from brilliant staff and much more about reliability and control. Work was still based around a set time and place. The human body was still largely a machine for moving things, perhaps lighter things with more dexterity, but as bodies primarily as muscles, not brains.

More than anything else, the entire world of business was still about production, about looking in on itself and perfecting the craft of making. It was rare for companies to commission market research to understand new needs; factories pushing out products dominated, and marketing became a tool that was bolted on as an afterthought. Today, most companies are still oriented around the factory. Most c-suite roles are about reducing the cost of goods, reducing the chance of litigation, improving factory conditions, and training staff better. Almost no companies actively look towards consumers as being the primary focus – they are simply the end destination.

## Era three – a focus on imagination and empathy

In 1959, business consultant Peter Drucker first coined the term 'knowledge work' in his book *The Landmarks of Tomorrow* (Drucker, 1959). He saw that value wasn't created simply by having workers produce goods or execute tasks; value was also created by workers' use of information. While technology amplifying our bodies enabled linear improvements in productivity, technology amplifying our minds could produce exponential improvements. Good ideas could be worth billions but cost nothing and take little time.

*Good ideas could be worth billions and cost nothing and take little time.*

As knowledge work grew as a proportion of the US and world economy, the new reality of managing knowledge and knowledge workers challenged all that organizations knew about management. The major component of the market value of the S&P 500 shifted dramatically from physical assets to intangible assets.

Suddenly working hours mattered less than the quality of those hours, the location where one worked seemed less relevant than the outputs that a place allowed. The proper relationship between manager and subordinate altered, communication became two-way, employee happiness became vital, not preferable. In knowledge-based work, physical assets become less dominant and relationships, intellectual property and reputations matter more. When all the value in an organization walks out the door each evening, a different managerial contract than the command-and-control mindset prevalent in execution-type work is required.

Thus, new theories of management arose that put far more emphasis on engagement, motivation, training, and perhaps even inspiration of workers. When knowledge workers are able to more easily move to different fields or countries, a lot of company effort is spent not just on recruitment but on retention.

Executives found their roles less about control, authority and documentation, and more about coaching. Leadership principles began to replace management.

Organizational theorists now study new theories like emotional intelligence, or working or learning styles. We now focus more on how people work together and how to attract brilliance more than conformity.

The very nature of what organizations are for and what purpose they serve is undergoing sweeping change.

Management has become about orchestration, about creating an environment in which people can be brilliant. Companies now compete on meaningful experiences for staff. The role of empathy has become core, both in terms of understanding and making what consumers want, but also in the nature of the employment contract. The power structure changes from a function of hierarchy to one of networks. Power no longer comes entirely from the top of hierarchies but from the centre of networks. Communication can flow in both directions; your email address may have the same rights to send as the boss's. We no longer need bureaucracy to carry messages. We move from hierarchies that are slow and cumbersome, burdened by record keeping, process, policy and bureaucracy, to small groups loosely connected, united by purpose, aligned and maintained by trust and reputation.

But even more important than empathy is the role of imagination. The power of a great idea is the most undervalued element in all business. Organizations still emphasize exploitation of existing advantages over creating new ones.

It is impossible to convey the significance of the changes required by the era of imagination.

Leaders now need to manage ambiguity, not conformity; they need to be predictive, not responsive. They need to create a market fit, not find and then satiate it. Companies increasingly outsource more and more non-core functions. Roles become about outsourcing and motivation, not monitoring and clarity. We now need width of talent, not reduction in the variety of people. We need training that doesn't make the same of everybody but makes the most of them. We need to find ways to create roles around (some) brilliant people, not squeeze them into organizational chart gaps.

Management and leadership of today and the future are becoming wildly different skills that rely on listening rather than talking, on imagination not engineering, on motivation not presence.

Institutions have been built to date on the principles and foundations of the past as for-profit entities. Senior management have often only ever worked in an environment where people never dreamed of liking their job, let alone finding purpose in it. As the world's young-

*What companies in the era of imagination are best at doing is rethinking the value proposition of an industry.*

est but best talent enters the workforce, we will find prospective talent dissatisfied with the idea of simply working to enrich others. Pursuing profit at the expense of the world's resources without consideration of a greater good is no longer attractive.

The brightest minds in talent management these days are starting to think of companies as being the entities that work for people; it is not their job to train people, but to support, motivate and inspire them to do it themselves. It is their job to provide people with the environment, equipment and capital they need to thrive in a role, and to ensure the barriers to progress are removed.

Huge challenges and opportunities exist in this environment. When work is done through networks rather than through lines of command, then how are people and projects managed? When work is unbundled from time and space, how do we know when people have been working hard enough? How do staff create work–life boundaries? If some roles should be developed around key people then how do we manage the average jealous staff? If more capable people are able to add three times more value, but work the same hours, how much more should we pay them? In many contemporary companies, what is really required is not dedication or hard work or even commitment or focus, but the magic of great ideas and persuasion. In many fields laziness is a useful way to create better ways to do things, but this can't reasonably be celebrated. In many creative industries compliance is less helpful than subversion. In most companies it's normally worse to have staff work there for too long and drag down others than to have staff that leave quickly after bursts of brilliance. What companies in the era of imagination are best at doing is rethinking the value proposition of an industry.

## New value propositions

Netflix is worth more than $300 billion at the time of writing, while at its peak in 2002, Blockbuster was worth $8.4 billion. I'm pretty sure while Reed Hastings was building the foundation for being the future of entertainment, senior staff at Blockbuster were negotiating for cheaper shelving units, doing deals to sell more

Pepsi, and discussing how to find more branches to open, while arguing with franchise owners about planograms for ice cream. If you take a step back, Netflix is in the business of entertaining people while Blockbuster was in the DVD rental business – one was clearly better.

So what business are you in? Who are your competitors? What is the role you have in people's lives? These are key questions that can unlock growth if you also raise your ambition level. And they don't sound too hard. Car makers make cars, hotels build, manage and operate rooms to stay in, clothing companies sell fashionable clothing – this seems easy.

Yet the problem with most companies is they tend to have a very functional, unimaginative and unambiguous view of what they do. They perfect what they do within the limited horizons of their competitor set. Consumer banks look at how other consumer banks make money, they don't look to China and what happens when consumers grow up without the same banking system. Hotels benchmark against hotels, not lifestyle or experiential brands. Car companies compare against other great engineers. Whether it comes to inspiration for better user experiences, or evaluating a competitor set, we need more imagination and, above all else, empathy.

Every day when we leave for work as a human being, we may feed the kids, worry about our savings, pay a gas bill, and remember we need to book a holiday soon. But then we go to work and remove our 'normal human being head' and put on the CEO or CFO, or Marketing Director or call centre operative or nurse head and lose track of what life is really like for people. In the real world we don't care about your brand values, we just care what it's like to work with you; we don't care about your vision statement, but we may be drawn to lovely packaging or a money-off coupon.

Yet companies obsess within their own worlds, and unnecessarily so. If you are a company that owns real estate in which you place gym equipment, then perhaps you'd be wiser to think of yourself as being in the business of making people healthier and happier. If nothing else, it would've allowed you to have survived the Covid-19 pandemic more easily. Are you an office provider like Regus, or are you in the business of 'creating happy productive teams'? The former allows you to make money from vending machines but take on risky leases, the latter allows you to become a technology platform that can rapidly scale around the world.

*These days value propositions can be more complex and murkier than ever.*

Quite a lot of companies have already got this; McDonald's and Pizza Hut are less restauranteurs than real estate owners. Four Seasons is less interested in land or hotel development but has rapidly become a lifestyle brand that sells franchises and does licensing deals. Boeing is really less of a plane maker and more of an engineering maintenance contract seller.

These days value propositions can be more complex and murkier than ever. Take a specific type of mobility, like access to cars. Any of these companies can claim to be in the space but they approach it from radically different directions:

- Uber is a marketplace to connect car owners and drivers with passengers.
- Tesla is a car assembler that makes money selling cars direct to people and from the software they download.
- BMW is a car maker that makes money selling cars via dealerships and on finance products and servicing.
- Turo is a marketplace that allows car owners to casually rent out their cars when not needed.
- Zipcar is a car rental firm that specializes in short-term and spontaneous car rental to drivers, but has no depot or storage locations.
- Hertz is a car rental firm that specializes in longer-term and planned car rental to drivers, operating from owned but mainly franchised depots.

Some of these operational starting points allow companies to be evaluated like tech companies. They allow faster expansion around the world, with fewer assets and lower levels of responsibility. Some are rooted in owning assets or brands. They all need rather different expertise despite being in the same 'business'.

For long periods of time, companies focused on what they knew to be important. People buy cars because of fuel efficiency, speed and looks. They stay in hotels because of nice sheets and posh toiletries, they choose the plane that's got the bigger seats, but times are changing.

I use a slower, more expensive train to visit my parents in the UK because it's got fast Wi-Fi and plug sockets. Now it's likely people select their car based on the entertainment system, how well it works with their phone and the experience of ownership, not the mechanical engineering that has long been perfected. An Audi owner told me recently that the best thing about their car is the app you can use to arrange the repair of scratches.

I now favour Delta over American because the app tells you when the flight boards, and it's honest and accurate. I choose Amazon to buy things because they make it easy to return items, not because they are cheaper. I ignore credit card providers with generous offers of Air Miles, speedy boarding and other 'expensive' perks, in favour of a card that lets me pay with contactless. I'd choose a car-riding service if it uploaded my receipts for faster expense processing. I'd choose a TV with a more attractive on-screen interface and a nicer remote. I choose Avis over Hertz now because you can change bookings in the app, not have to call someone over the phone who won't ever answer and if they do will be tapping away for ever to tell you they don't know.

The issue is that companies look in on themselves. They are driven by passions that drew people to work there, they don't reflect consumer needs and wishes. The engineers at Mercedes take great delight in eking out an extra MPG from a diesel engine, but Tesla engineers made 'dog mode' because they realized a benefit of electric cars was that the air conditioning can run even when the car isn't running. Dog mode is a mode where you can leave a dog, or I guess any other creature, in the car on a hot day and know that the temperature is maintained to keep them cool. It also displays on a large screen 'the dog is OK', so dog lovers don't smash windows in panic. It does not, I believe, feed dogs.

Companies work around their culture, priorities and experience, not consumer empathy. A train company may obsess over on-time performance as an engineering-led logistics firm, but not cabin design or Wi-Fi or real-time info as a point of difference. Amazon takes an obsessive approach as a logistics company caring about price and reliability, not ease of ordering, or using data and marketing to seduce people into buying things they don't need, or even employing staff to ensure products sold have a degree of quality and curation.

Design and customer service become far more important and differentiating in the digital age, where switching costs are minimal and customers are overserved. Banks over the years have spent countless billions on ensuring an incredibly impressive and trustworthy high-street presence, and millions on marketing and brand building, but offered a nicely designed mobile app and a quick sign-up process, customers may move fast. I choose to pay money to a private doctor because I can make appointments via an app. I use my Amex credit card despite it giving me fewer points per purchase, because if I want to dispute a charge, it lets me do it in seconds online.

## Don't be in a dying value proposition

Whenever there is a death of a large company, people use existing simplistic narratives to explain it. People always think there is a 'reason companies fail' when in fact it's that all companies die, unless great decisions and hard work keep them afloat. We should be amazed at how long companies routinely stay solvent rather than shocked when a company goes under. No brand or entity has a right to survive.

Many companies fail because their value proposition no longer makes sense. Department stores in particular are based on the old-world behaviour that we need somewhere close by to sell us things and the unit economics of the past favoured this, but compare this with AO.com.

Just imagine, if there was no such thing as John Lewis or Macy's or Sears or Toys"R"Us, would someone try to create it today? Top Shop didn't die because 'it failed to invest in digital', it failed because the dynamics of retail for young, price-sensitive shoppers, who want to wear what's cool, suit a totally different model based on e-commerce to circumvent high retail outlet costs, influencers who now can be the arbiters and spreaders of taste, real-time inventory and drop shipping, not renting expensive real estate, ordering vast sums of clothing up front and paying people money to sell it.

When Toys"R"Us failed, it was blamed on Amazon. What people failed to understand was that in 2020, you don't want to be a toy retailer but you do want to be an experience creator like Disney, or a digital-first logistics operation like Amazon. Something that wasn't possible when Toys"R"Us accepted the terms of a management buyout that demanded huge loan repayment costs that crippled its ability to invest in quality staff, training or brilliant fun store experiences.

## New core competencies

If the centre of your value proposition no longer retains relevance, you need to change the business that you are in. If the world presents itself with amazing new opportunities to explore, you need to change the skillset that you employ.

Both of these approaches require one of the hardest things in business, a change of core competency. In a 1990 article titled 'The Core Competence of the Corporation', the term Core Competency was coined by the professors Gary Hamel and CK Prahalad (Prahalad and Hamel, 1990). They called it 'a harmonized combination of multiple resources and skills that distinguish a firm in the marketplace'. Core competencies are, in the alleged words of Mark Ritson, the esteemed outspoken former professor of marketing at Melbourne Business School, 'the sh*t you do best' – I think I prefer this definition.

One may expect that if Starbucks, a maker of coffee-inspired products around the world, wanted to sell drinks in grocery stores, it wouldn't be so hard. But it turns out they are happy to be paid $7.1 billion by Nestlé for perpetual global rights to market and make Starbucks products to be sold outside of their stores, because the two identical things are very different (CNBC, 2018).

Starbucks' customers are consumers, Nestlé's customers are retailers. Opening a new store every 15 hours for five years, every day, means that Starbucks is essentially a real-estate company, while Nestlé is the world's largest food company, with a focus on packaging, distribution and advertising, like every other FMCG/CPG company out there.

For quite some time industries have generally been made up of companies with similar core competencies.

Samsung, Sharp and LG may decide to go about OLED TVs with different technologies behind them, but they are all great at stuff to do with tiny electronics, making things smaller, cheaper, lighter, brighter. They are all utterly disastrous at having any idea what people want, hence weird missteps into 3D TVs and then, most bizarrely, curved TVs.

Typically, when we see companies sell a wider variety of items, it's not brands or core competencies, but licensing. The Aston Martin Residences in Miami are not a new skillset for a British car maker but a marketing partnership. Armani may appear to make Armani hotels, eyewear, watches and perfume, but these are from Emaar Properties, Luxottica, Fossil and L'Oréal. Luxury brands in particular are brand-making companies.

Focus is key, and as strategic leader Michael Porter says, 'The essence of strategy is choosing what not to do' (Porter, 1996). Often what great companies have in common is focusing on a smaller set of activities, to a tighter vision of your company's reason to exist.

It seems likely that the reason IKEA has come so slowly to online retail is that they are happy to be a company rooted in logistics, real estate and great product design, and really as a retailer. Anyone who has witnessed and survived buying or most of all returning an item to IKEA knows how they treat their customers: we are the end point of their logistics process. The lack of enthusiasm to sell online shows their obsession with costs and spreadsheets, not making life better for their customer base. Amazon seem obsessed with figuring out how to deliver items to people as fast and cheaply and possible, but less interested in making sure using the website is a joy, or that goods sold are in any way adding delight to their customers. When you let X amount of people sell online, you end up with companies using artificial intelligence to make myriad phone covers or motivational posters, in the hope one may one day sell.

In particular, in this current time the great divide in business seems to be the skillset, mindset and experience in either software or hardware. Generally, all of the main legacy companies we typically think of (outside of software companies like Microsoft) are brilliant at manufacturing, selling or distributing physical things or services, and generally totally useless at customer-facing software.

## Tech will set you free!

Yet the painful truth is that focusing on making things and not technology can not only limit your company's valuations but limit its growth potential. I met the founder of a brilliant startup in the retail space in Sweden recently and while their unmanned walk-in grocery stores are a brilliant solve for the space left in rural Sweden when grocery stores close in sparsely populated areas and where labour costs are high, the reality is that in order to scale fast, building a platform that can retrospectively make existing retailers more efficient is a better way to grow fast and turn a profit.

If tech is your core competency then you may be able to transcend categories FAR more easily and quickly. Klarna can be a lender, a bank, a data provider, a secure login, from its starting point as a payment app. Spotify can move from music to podcasts, to theoretically be a TV provider or a seller of concert tickets; Airbnb can morph from the provision of spare beds to a provider of any human-to-human experience. If you run Google maps there is no reason you can't sell products, movie tickets, arrange dental appointments, book tee times on golf courses, or flights, or literally anything in the world. These are thin, delightful, user-friendly brands that provide a gateway to an endless array of services. And when you are an app that is trusted, on the homepage of hundreds of millions of phones, your ability to drive traffic and make money is unprecedented, so long as you do it well.

## Spanning hardware and software

'Hardware is hard. It's called hardware for a reason' is apparently an utterance by Marc Andreessen in 2013 (Kelleher, 2017). And yet despite being funded to the eyeballs and staffed by the precocious, large software companies have shown how their skillset rarely works.

You can pick pretty much any large consumer-oriented tech company and see the struggles they have making physical products in all directions. The Facebook Phone (actually made by

HTC) was an unloved device that failed to sell in any significant quantities, and their recent products like the Facebook Portal show no signs of any remote commercial success.

Tech companies seem driven by their digital product roadmap and repeatedly show few signs of consumer knowledge, or at least an understanding of people who are not rather extreme fans of all things technology. The failure of the ridiculous Snap Spectacles (twice now) seems to demonstrate both enthusiasm and determination, but also an almost undignified lack of understanding of their target audience or, perhaps, any human being.

## True agnosticism

My favourite question to ask someone who speaks two or more languages fluently is what language they dream in. We all have a leading hand. Similarly, we could ask what language companies use as their predominant culture. Software or hardware?

Making cigarettes is not something that on the face of it seems likely to be a fast-changing swirl of action and disruption. Tobacco companies like Philip Morris have long perfected the art of procuring quality tobacco from around the world, dealing with complex international arrangements for growing and importing tobacco, and (like it or not) have done a miraculous job of advertising and marketing in a world that is slowly making it hard for them. For them the 'smoking industry' is about the creation and distribution of cigarettes; they are steeped in consumer research, archetypes, media mixes and the tools of a company that knows how to sell stuff.

In many ways their expertise gets in the way. For a company like Juul, or HQD, NJOY or Blu, cigarette smoking is really about a nicotine rush, and an electronic device like a vape or e-cigarette is a much more effective (perhaps now even cooler) way to get the hit.

Yet take a look at the job listings for these companies and they are seeking wildly different talent. Battery engineers, heating coil specialists, electrical engineers, product designers. These are companies solving 'the problem' in a wildly different way. And yet when global behemoth Philip Morris entered the 'smokeless' world of vaping, it did so with IQOS, a device that looks rather like a vape but heats up tobacco. They somehow seemed determined to enter the evolved and fast-changing landscape, with their leadership position in distribution, by making something that still relied on growing tobacco. It seems we let our core competencies hold us back.

Large, dominant companies seem deeply reluctant to change what they do best. Petrol stations around the world are closing and the need to charge electric vehicles is skyrocketing, so it seems smart to expect oil companies to undertake a pretty swift and smooth conversion of forecourts to charging stations but it's not really happening. From an outsider perspective it seems the core competency of energy companies running petrol forecourts was in transporting fuel safely, a logistics challenge that met the consumer at a nice place to buy coffee and pump up tires. In reality, in the future, when electric cars may take 20+ minutes to charge, the core competency needed for 'refilling' stations, while seemingly the same need state for consumers, is something more akin to operating an amusement arcade or cinema, or even a big retail chain. How can you drive traffic and make money from people's time while keeping them happy? In a similar way, if car makers are to move to making electric vehicles, a key problem to solve will be range anxiety and the software that makes it easy to plan routes that allow the owners to charge the most quickly, with the shortest possible detour. Something a company like Uber or Google is way better tooled to resolve than a mechanical engineering company with a history of celebrating wonderful gas mileage and smooth gear changes.

## The power of ideas

While we've always focused on ourselves and how to make what we make better, the third management age offers us a new lens through which to think about what we do – the vantage point of the consumer. People want cars that are a delight to own and drive and this includes the quality of interiors and well-fitted body panels, powerful engines, the feeling of the logo on our keys and what the brand represents, but also now the ease at which we can refill and the hassle in buying, selling and servicing the car. We are now in the business of both software and hardware but also experiences and services.

For too long we've been obsessed with the idea that technology needs to be advanced or new, that things need to BE objectively better, but increasingly they need to FEEL better. This includes how we buy things, what it's like to unbox them, return them, receive them.

We've also begun to conflate the term innovation with 'technology'. We presume the innovation is the application of something advanced; it's the camera and digital screen on the smart fridge that lets us look inside, rather than a fridge with a see-through door. It's making a curved TV screen, not finding a simple way to rejig the parts inside existing TVs to make them fit against the wall more tightly. Innovation in particular always seems to involve adding something.

The third industrial age is about design, it's about understanding people and their needs. Innovation has become about something new or a change made to an existing product, idea or field. But it should be about better. And better often requires thought more than engineering, reductions not addition, and this requires companies to really rethink and reimagine what they make, and the way they are structured. This typically involves a degree of transformation based around the possibilities of technology, but also the evolved needs and altered behaviours of the digital age – a topic explored in the next chapter.

CHAPTER FIVE

# Starting your digital transformation

*The secret of change is to focus all of your energy, not on fighting the old, but on building the new.*
DAN MILLMAN

The colourful signage on the American Airlines lounge in Miami seemed rather promising: 'We are reimagining your lounge.' When it opened it was perfectly nice; it had new carpets, new seating, a flatter TV, some new 'nobody could ever take offence' art, but that was it. We had a word for this before 2020: 'refurbished'. Similarly, the local branch of Bank of America has opened after undergoing a well-publicized 'digital transformation'; it turned out this meant super comfy sofas and a coffee shop. Now don't get me wrong, I love bland art, I adore soft furnishings and I need coffee near me at all times, but these were all examples of our love of the press release, and the difficult reality of deeper change. It does appear that in a world of sparkling rhetoric and buzzwords, it's become essential to merchandise change, and to do it fast and easily, over actually changing, and this is something that plagues digital transformation initiatives.

## A metaphor for business

Modern businesses can be visualized as skyscrapers. They exist on vast, deep foundations, built in the shape and with techniques that the best thinking at the time suggested. The location of the skyscraper's foundation is set by optimizing local and global knowledge, economic forces, and a sprinkling of what's been learned through years of best practice.

From this foundation, a steel or concrete frame thrusts into the air, forming the main structural elements and defining the building's shape and function. Fixed into place around the main structure are the service elements and windows and interior walls. In a skyscraper, these could be the lifts, fire escapes, service corridors and the networks for water, electricity and so on.

Finally, with the building watertight, topped out and left as a raw space to use, the more visible, decorative elements are installed. This is interior design: the funky office furniture, the marble in the lobby, the artwork in the toilets, the corporate film that plays in reception and the small details that best shape the visitor's experience.

Companies are like this. The interior design is what the company does to represent itself: marketing, branding, press releases, advertising... everything that is the outermost of what a company does. This is what people see most readily; it's the most superficial aspect of design, but also what most efficiently represents what the company wants to be. We can wallpaper over cracks, we can distract attention if need be. For both the building and the business it represents, it's this visual garnish, this accessible layer, that is both the easiest thing to change as well as the most illusory. It's an efficient way of changing appearance, rather than what matters more fundamentally.

The fit-out, the walls, windows and service elements represent the culture and processes of business today. Harder to alter, easily visible. They are the way that a building and a business operate, the lifeblood that makes it work. The skyscraper's frame is a metaphor for a company's organizational form. Frames are the organizational elements: the departmental structures, the rules, the core elements of operations. They are what you can see, but are often hidden, and rarely inspected or cared about.

And then there are the foundations, the base that supports everything, the invisible but vital core element to centre everything. This is the business model, the role of the company, the reason it exists.

So, in a world undergoing profound change, what does a business do when it discovers it's not in the right place? What if our skyscraper made sense in London, but now should be in São Paulo? What if we don't need to house 1,000 workers and we've constructed something too tall? What if we need very different spaces? Like skyscrapers, most companies can easily change their appearance, but not their structure. They can invest in great works of art to show off, or distract, but they can rarely alter what they are about and built for. The reality is that the most central, structural and vital elements are almost impossible to even consider changing, so then what do we do?

In fact, the world of construction offers many metaphors for businesses. The UK has spent billions of pounds maintaining old train lines, rather than building new high-speed lines. The business case for a massive injection of capital was too hard. Today's expensive, slow and at-capacity train lines are the result of years of incremental change, a steady, more palatable flow of investment. The old, maintained train lines still exist because the work could be done continuously rather than taking 10 years to build – and disruption would therefore be minimized. However, it's really because nobody had the courage to make a difficult decision that would have taken a long time to show results.

The shifting nature of business has created an environment of change where modern business models, new technologies, new consumer behaviours and new competitors mean that the large, lumbering infrastructure of established businesses increasingly looks like the wrong thing, built in the wrong place.

Today, new companies that are built on new thinking, systems, code, technology and culture are making their older equivalents look archaic. Why develop software in-house when you can outsource to specialists? Why try to craft bespoke units when philosophies like containerization or systems like Kubernetes are effectively prefabricated units that can be easily dropped in? Why own when you can rent, like SAAS? In fact, the architecture of software has changed radically, with developments like advanced APIs allowing integrations to be far more important than the elements you make and maintain yourselves. The digital world is one where you construct a framework of instructions to pull things from different places, rather than building everything yourself.

These legacy issues are clearly not just software issues, they manifest themselves in very different ways and at very different scales. Retailers that wish they didn't own stores. Entertainment companies that wish they'd bought global rights when they made content. Car companies that wish they'd not invested in billion-dollar combustion engine plants, or dealership networks. I often see successful but empty restaurants and wonder if the owners just wish that they could use Seamless or Grubhub and not rent a vast space where people once sat. The role of these businesses has shifted, but it's hard for them to accept they are not where they wish they were.

We have banks that don't want to be tied to the regulation of what being a bank actually is. Airlines wish that they didn't have unionized workers or gasoline-burning older fleets. Most importantly, many companies now wish that they did not own factories, or distribution centres, or perhaps employ as many workers.

The degree of change required, the company's location, the expense, time and risk involved in making these changes mean that paralysis strikes as well as pride. And every year that passes, the pressure grows. Every deteriorating, unvisited department store anchoring the shopping centre, every DVD rental kiosk, every tired bank branch, acting as anchors that make change harder.

But where do you go from here? How do you keep the attributes that made you succeed for so long and add what you need? Is it really the case that you need to start again? And what if you are a successful company that needs to change course, or a startup that needs to pivot? These questions all get to the heart of what digital transformation is really about, something I will now define.

## What does digital transformation mean?

Digital transformation is not an especially easy term to explain or define clearly, partly because it's made up of two vague terms. Transformation itself is just to go about 'marked change in form, nature, or appearance', and therefore lends itself to being misused. Digital is equally useless, as it means 'involving or relating to the use of computer technology'. Digital has come to feel like a noun, verb, adverb and adjective at the same time. In theory, if you change your logo on a website you've gone about a digital transformation.

In my opinion 'transformation' is about the substantiveness of a change made. It's about the depth, profoundness and implications of what has been done. The degree to which assumptions have been challenged and the extent to which all questions have been posed and parameters altered.

Digital is best explained in terms of a wide set of implications; my favourite explanation of the notion of digital is:

> Applying the culture, practice, processes and technologies of
> the Internet era, to respond to people's raised expectations.
> (Loosemore, 2016)

What I love about this quote is not just its simplicity but the degree to which it refers to the broader changing environment in which we operate. What it addresses is the idea of technology as a culture, and it seems to refer to changing consumer expectations, as well as the new possibilities it affords.

## Important things that are too important to change

One of the great ironies of the modern age is that the more important something is, the less likely it's been digitally transformed. It is the scale and the vitalness of the system that make it most overwhelming and least desirable to take on. Netflix may have entirely rethought the way we make, distribute, license and consume entertainment (which, despite how brilliant many shows are, isn't an essential service), but healthcare systems remain disjointed and archaic. We may have new retailers and distribution systems like Amazon or Ocado, but finding and buying a home remains a total mess. Cars from makers like Lucid or Tesla or even the Ford Mach-e may be built from the ground up, but education, government, the welfare state, the armed forces are legacy systems where change has been least forthcoming, for a variety of reasons.

Perhaps the very most important computer system on the planet, and one on which many of the world's lives depend, is the Strategic Automated Command and Control System (SACCS). It's a system used within the US military to allow command centres to send emergency action messages to field forces. This system, until 2018, used 8-inch floppy disks and antiquated 1970s computers (IBM Series/1) to receive nuclear launch orders from the President (Stack, 2019). Which is quite a thought.

While the Fukushima nuclear plant triple meltdowns in 2011 weren't directly caused by software, many have said that the power plant running on Windows XP, a 20-year-old operating system, didn't exactly help. This wasn't surprising because Tokyo Electric Power Company (TEPCO) had over 48,000 PCs running this outdated software, with security updates and other vital patches not available after Microsoft stopped the version seven years ago (Whitwam, 2015). We see critical systems everywhere, even newly built 'best in class' fancy pants stuff.

Computer systems are rather like Rome. A city built on another city, on an older city, and in fact so many iterations of cities that nobody really knows any more. Rather large lintels holding up the windows on your quaint Airbnb off Piazza di Spagna may have been recycled many times over, as is the case with much of the city. We need not worry what it was, or how it works, we just need to know that it does.

In fact, much of the world is built on the oldest foundations, with the most archaic parts possible. One of the very oldest programming languages around today, COBOL, developed in the 1950s, still has 220 billion lines of code in active use. The main users of it are banks and other financial institutions, where 43 per cent of banking systems use COBOL. Transportation systems and government agencies are other key users of this wildly outdated software, with increasingly few software engineers trained to use it. In the United States, the Department of Justice, Treasury Department, Department of Homeland Security and Social Security Administration all have systems that rely in some part on COBOL (McKay, 2020).

This may indeed be great code, but the issue is that people know that these systems work but not how. They create systems prone to failure. In February 2021 it emerged from the Arizona Department of Corrections that hundreds of incarcerated people who should have been eligible for release were being held in prison because the inmate management software couldn't interpret current sentencing laws. After an amendment to state law that was passed in 2019, one of the software modules within ACIS (Arizona Correctional Information System) designed to calculate release dates for inmates wasn't able to reduce sentences based on new laws. A system that some say has more than 14,000 bugs seems to ruin lives because replacing the system is deemed too expensive. Instead, prison employees have been manually counting early release dates for nearly two years (Cox, 2021).

It should not be a surprise that these archaic systems create problems, rather like using ancient Roman pipes as structural beams, as they were developed for a different use, and for an era where the internet didn't exist, cybersecurity wasn't a thing, where code was designed to not be updated regularly and, most of all, where data storage was assumed to be expensive.

## Legacy foundations are everywhere and reduce what we can build on top

On 10 March 2021, respected medical journal *The Lancet* caused shock around the world when it discovered in Spain that the child mortality rate from Covid-19 was 4.9 per cent for kids between the ages of 10 and 19, with 28 kids under 9 years old dying with Covid. Since the start of the pandemic the Spanish Ministry of Health reports had been used for guidance around lockdowns and school closures in the country. Yet it turned out that the input box on the software used to gather reports was again only two digits long, so anyone over the age of 100 wouldn't be registered as such; a 102-year-old would be registered as aged two (Debré, 2021).

## Why are vital systems so hard to change?

There are many reasons for the cruel contrast between a system's importance and its degree of outdatedness.

Generally speaking, the most important systems around are older. They've had years to calcify, to grow, to have scope change, and they become an amalgam of fixes, kludges, workarounds, middleware and other added-on elements. New generations of code sit on top of older legacy foundations. It's easy for Uber or Monzo, Lemonade or Netflix to use modern programming languages and code when these companies have simply not been around that long. It's older companies like eBay or British Airways where you see older foundations and designs appear a few clicks into the website.

Vital systems tend to be larger. A healthcare system like the UK's National Health Service (NHS), which is the world's fifth-largest employer, must work for 1.7 million employees and 1.37 million PCs. Software must span everything from procurement to payroll to managing complex 3D images to calendar management (Smith, 2019). The enormous scope of outputs, the aged legacy foundations and the sheer size of the system create a complexity that few can begin to tackle. As a result, perhaps nobody actually understands how the system works, only that it does. They learn empirical fixes, like 'have you tried turning it off and on again?', and dare not change any fundamental base element as the knock-on effects are unknown.

Because of the vitalness of these systems there is the need to be always on or with 'high availability'. These are systems or components that need to be operational without interruption for long periods of time and with minimal downtime. A 100 per cent system is a system that never fails; more realistically, 99.99 per cent, or 'four nines', is considered excellent uptime. The very most important systems for our lives therefore have a reduced ability to ever be taken out of service for crucial upgrades. The classic Silicon Valley line 'build the plane while flying it' becomes a useful metaphor, or at least 'repair it as it's flying'.

But most of all, these systems are secondary to the main driver and culture of the workforce. Few of the world's best IT folk would be lured into the NHS in the UK, and there are not many tech wizards and wannabe billionaires who dream of working for the military. Why would you seek to join a place where the common culture is not celebrating the importance of what you do when places like Google, Pinterest, Shopify, or even IBM are the cathedrals to your religion?

The military needs a workforce aligned around expertise in warfare, mechanical engineering, military strategy, and thus software and information technology have remained far from core competencies. Healthcare is rooted in a culture around medicine and medical expertise, not one drawn to considering project management of software projects as vital. Leaders of such entities have grown up as figureheads for their subject matter, sharing their vantage points and their knowledge. They are unlikely to consider code or digital devices as core to their future strategy.

To understand how digital transformation or any other change happens, it's best to consider how companies or government departments or even people really work, and to do this we need to look at their architecture.

## Onions

There is a theory in social science that the characteristics and attributes of people can be best represented by a stacked Euler diagram, or more easily visualized as an onion. The work in social penetration theory, started by Irwin Altman and Dalmas Taylor, suggests that people are based around concentric layers, with the most superficial and visible behaviours on the edge, and the innermost and existential at the heart or core.

The easiest aspect of people to see is behaviour, the outermost layer. A little deeper in the onion is our knowledge and skills. The next layer within the onion is our attitudes. These are the core ways in which we think about the world, how we tend to behave and how we understand and make sense of the world. They are our default ways of dealing with situations and are typically built upon our values – the next layer in.

Our values are deep. They develop slowly over time in response to our experiences. Values take months or years to change. Values are central to who we are as a person. They are a representation of how we make decisions, how we go about our life. These are the very foundational elements of who we are.

FIGURE 5.1 The conceptual layers of a company

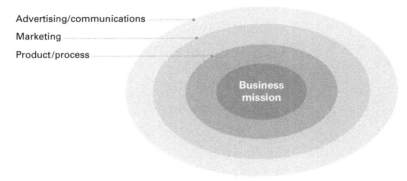

Companies are not analogous to people, but the example of onions works well to better understand the structure of businesses, what drives them to be what they are, and what layers make them up. Figure 5.1 illustrates this concept of multi-layered companies.

So imagine your business as an onion, as a series of concentric layers around a small core, each and every layer built on top of the next innermost layer. We can start to make sense of the complex structures of businesses and how they do everything from finding meaning to making products, creating and supporting brands. The following section, which moves from the outermost to the innermost layers, illustrates the similarities between personality traits and business traits.

## The communications layer: the outermost layer

For businesses, people's behaviour equates to the communications they put out: the paid-for, controlled messages of advertising and the websites they own, or the brand's and the business's PR strategy. These are the environments where companies proactively decide what the world or their target audience should think of them. They are the places where the company gets to control most tightly 'the message' and most precisely visualize and make real 'the brand'. This layer explains to the world what it is that a company makes. Communications can be:

- owned media like websites and stores, brochures, blogs, or email newsletters;
- earned media like reviews, PR, organic search;
- paid media, which is primarily what we've always thought of as advertising – paid media placements where the business gets to control the message entirely.

## The marketing layer: supporting communications

Supporting the communications layer would be the marketing layer, a much more diverse array of activities that a company undertakes to both sell products and create the brand. You could argue that it is this layer that creates the full meaning of brand and the full understanding in a consumer's mind of what a product or service is, what it means, what it's worth and more. This layer includes:

- Place: the geographical location where the product is offered, the type of distribution channel used and increasingly the strategy behind distribution – placement both in terms of where the product is for sale, as well as the context and precise location within the store or online where the product is found.
- Pricing: the amount a customer pays for a product or the sacrifice or effort people are prepared to make to acquire a product.
- Promotion: generally, the sum of all marketing communications is to make the offer or brand known and understood to potential and current customers in order to persuade them to take an interest or buy the product. This is generally understood to include advertising, PR, sales promotion, direct marketing, and increasingly, influencer marketing, owned media, sponsorship and a dazzling array of new techniques or

even old techniques which for some reason are considered new again, like branded content or native advertising. It's this part of the marketing layer that the outermost communications layer most directly builds on.

## The product layer: what you make

The product layer is the 'what' of a company: the part of the business that is the manifestation of its reason for existence. It is the product or service it makes, but in the broadest terms. Products are increasingly deemed to be more than just their tangible physicality.

Products encompass everything that you experience as an owner or user. They include all touchpoints: the check-in desk at the airport; the clerk at the bank; the form you fill in to get insurance and the terms and conditions, labelling and merchandising of the policy. Products run deep. For example, in cars they include the after-sales service, the emails before your lease ends – the feeling of ownership in its totality.

## The operations layer: the how

The operations layer is the 'how' of a company: everything that gets things made. It includes the process and structure, technology and culture of a company. From how people are expected to behave, to how and why people are recruited, the training they undertake, and the spirit and attitudes they are likely to have and represent. Is the company autocratic, democratic or (unlikely) holacratic? How do they come up with new ideas, how do they budget for R&D?

It covers culture too. Are people empowered to make decisions or are they hiding in a culture of fear? Does the company seek to outsource as much as possible or keep control? The how includes process: the organizational chart, the way decisions get made, how meetings are arranged, how people are judged and supported, promoted and fired. It covers systems too, the technology used to underpin a company. Does it use Slack, Dropbox, video-conferencing software? What are the security features like? Is the company open-plan or tucked away in cubicles? Is it open or closed minded?

## Mission or business model: the core

'What does your company exist to do?' is a pretty bold question and one we need to ask more. If your company vanished tomorrow, what would people miss? What is the role you fulfil in the world?

This is not the 'why' – we need to escape that fallacy. This is more brutal and commercial, it's how you make money, it's the business model. It's hard to understate the importance of the mission, yet few companies have a clearly defined one, outside of hyperbole and generic copywriting.

If Nike says, 'If you have a body, you are an athlete' and that their role is to 'bring inspiration and innovation to every athlete in the world', then you know what you are supposed to be doing and not doing when you work there. If IKEA stands for 'making everyday life better for our customers with well-designed products', it's pretty empowering. The mission is the raison d'être; it's how people focus, celebrate, prioritize. The mission of the company is what supports everything else. It drives and reinforces the culture and processes, which then design, refine and make the products and experiences, which are then communicated to the market.

## Applying digital transformation to this model

So if we take the definition of digital transformation as 'applying the culture, practice, processes and technologies of the internet era to respond to people's raised expectations', a great question is, how does this relate to our onion?

We get new questions. How deeply are you applying new technology? What is the new context in which you now operate? What new consumer behaviours can you work around and leverage?

## It's easiest to innovate closest to the edge

The outermost (communications) layer offers the easiest possible innovation. It requires the least organizational effort, the most superficial of conversations, is easiest and fastest to achieve and is the most highly visible. Not least because the budget and control are normally within one department.

It is most desirable too. Innovation at the communications layer is the fastest, most efficient way to show the world you're ahead of the industry. Deliver a can of Coke to construction workers in Jakarta with a drone and stick the video on YouTube. Job done. Place a vending machine in a shopping mall in Dubai and give free ice creams to those who smile, make a case study video, overlay some U2 – and celebrate at Cannes. Take a picture of your advert and sell it as an NFT, get your PR agency to get someone to buy it for $100k and bow to great applause.

Communications innovation in the digital age just requires embracing new platforms, new gadgets, new startups – and away we go. Innovation at this level is normally pretty cheap, involves few stakeholders internally, can be outsourced to agencies, and is quite easy to get a budget for. If you want to spend $50,000 on a chatbot, the money comes quite quickly as the PR results can usually be easily measured to show success. If you want to give a Blockchain startup $25,000 to try something with a loyalty card, or $100,000 for a VR experience at a tradeshow, then you won't need to reach far upstream into your client's complex organizational politics. In fact, you can probably get rewarded with some decent press merely for announcing an intent to do something. Especially with Blockchain or AI, because few people really know what they are.

The problem is that it rarely makes a difference to the bottom line. It's all innovation for innovation's sake, never or rarely to make a difference.

## Innovation at the marketing level

Innovation at the marketing layer makes a bigger difference, and is slightly harder to bring about. Dollar Shave Club, Warby Parker, Away suitcases, Allbirds shoes, Casper and Wayfair are examples of companies that have considered new ways to go to market, new ways to price or distribute, but they don't sell things especially different from before. They have gone against many industry norms, but are not, at the core, radically different companies to their predecessors, and they are all new 'tech'-centric companies and not transformed older companies.

Walmart offer key glimpses into how this can be done. They've genuinely rethought a lot of their business for the modern age. Offering ways for people to buy online and pick up instore, they've redesigned their stores to make this easier and trained new staff on how to work this way.

We see hotel chains, due to the rise of travel search engines and platforms, changing how they price rooms to be far more dynamic. No longer are prices based on peak, off-peak and shoulder seasons, but on real-time demand and inventory levels.

## The product layer: what you make

Applying digital transformation thinking at the product layer becomes harder and thus rarely still.

The world may offer a variety of new products constructed for this age: the Nest thermostat, the iRobot vacuum, Oculus headsets, Rent the Runway, or other everyday item rental services like Fat Llama, or even pay-as-you-go car insurance like Metromile.

When it comes to existing companies transforming, there are cases like HSBC creating First Direct to reimagine banking, or BMW making its electrically propelled iSeries or offering car-sharing services via DriveNow, or hotel chain Premier Inn creating Zip, a hotel brand based around contemporary needs and behaviours. We can look at Microsoft using its skills and expertise to make Xbox. Boeing have changed the way they sell their products so that most customers now buy service contracts on engines rather than the engines alone. But these are all new offerings, incremental add-ons to an existing business, and very small in scope compared to the longer-term business.

However, the examples of companies transforming what they make are very limited.

## Applying new thinking at the process layer: the how

Going deeper into the core of the business, we now consider those companies that apply new thinking and new technology to the product and process layer.

The 'how' is the process and systems behind how you do business. McDonald's managed to implement a new digital kiosk system as well as online ordering from phones, which required relatively deep backend integration into their entire operational system in every (or most) branch(es). This had significant implications on the workflow behind the scenes and was an impressive demonstration of how these things can create value for customers. Ordering from a mobile app allows you to join a different queue in-store, and pick up goods remarkably fast. Digital kiosks allow you to place an order that gets delivered to your table. Both have radically changed the customer experience.

AstraZeneca went through the process of outsourcing much of their innovation and streamlining that work to focus on their core competency. Now much of the more ambitious new product development is done by universities or other research bodies, radically changing their cost structure.

But again, demonstrations of this type of thinking are rather unusual and even the McDonald's example above is stretching the definition.

## Deeper transformation: companies with new thinking at the core

The companies that are truly different are those that have applied new thinking and new technology, and have worked around new customer behaviours and expectations at the very core of their business. They have taken tech to the very heart of what they do.

The examples are clear and notable and include for example Amazon, Alibaba, Facebook, Google. But you will know that these are not companies that have transformed, merely companies that have built themselves from scratch for the new era.

Netflix is perhaps the most dramatic example of a company that went through deeply radical change right to the very centre of the business. Reid Hoffman realized that the business and logistics of sending DVDs through the mail to customers was unlikely to be a long-term winner at the time the internet was rapidly evolving. Rather than tweak the business model he decided to completely transform the entire fundamental structure and assumptions beneath the business, first to embrace the power of streaming and to change the way the customers were charged for movies, and once again in more recent times to shift to being not just the distributor of entertainment but the maker of it. When doing this Netflix ensured that they procured global rights across all media, all markets and for perpetuity, allowing them total flexibility to move into any market and do many different things.

IBM is another often-quoted example. They moved from the business of selling computer equipment to the business of consulting, but in some ways this was less of a transformation and more of a retreat from a category facing huge competitive pressure and a slightly lost vision.

## How to transform your company

The next four chapters outline a four-step process which I believe is best suited to companies and how they can approach and bring about meaningful and transformative change:

- **Step One: Provoking transformation**
  Here we look at the steps that are required to establish the need for urgency and appetite for change.
- **Step Two: Creating a vision and mission for the future**
  Here we look at the steps needed to create a bold but relevant and empowering vision for change, one that is ambitious but practical, as we outline broad strategies for realigning around this.
- **Step Three: Operational transformation**
  This part looks at the process and structure needed to best transform. It details how technology now allows companies to operate in vastly different ways, and how innovation can be bought, borrowed, or built. It gives you the chance to envision your ideal operating system, then outlines steps for getting there.
- **Step Four: The culture for digital transformation**
  Change isn't a one and done approach, and it's notably hard to accomplish. The fourth and final step, and perhaps the most important one, is about creating a self-sustaining approach to new thinking, motivated workers, and is designed to ensure continual reinvention through a new culture creation.

Let me be very clear that this is only something that comes last in the process because it's very hard to do it before the infrastructure and environment for change are put in place. It is without doubt a vital element for any transformation and the one guaranteed to ensure it will not only succeed but be sustained and renewed for the future.

**FAILURE CASE STUDY** Boeing and the perils of tweaking

The Boeing 737 was the world's best-selling plane for five decades, until Airbus took over with the A320 in 2019, aided significantly by entirely rethought planes with much larger and more fuel-efficient engines. It was the spring of 2011 when Boeing took a call from American Airlines, an exclusive Boeing customer for more than a decade, which was about to defect to Airbus.

Aware they were running behind and had been complacent with the 737, Boeing made a huge decision, not to develop a new passenger plane from scratch, which would take a decade, but instead to take six years to radically update the 737. Boeing had not only its future business with American on the line, but pride – Airbus had been delivering more jets than Boeing for several years.

Faced with tight timelines, engineers were pushed to submit designs at double the normal pace, but also to limit the changes made to the airframe. If the plane was to be designed, built and, crucially, certified quickly, and to reduce any pilot retraining, the alterations had to be as minimal as possible. The goal was speed, not perfection. The cockpit was upgraded to a digital display, but rather than rethink the design for the best user interface, digital gauges replaced old analogue gauges nearly perfectly to reduce changes in training and manuals.

Originally designed in 1968, the low-to-the-ground design was a plus back then as it carried its own staircase; the Boeing 737-100 had folding metal stairs attached to the fuselage that passengers climbed to board before airports had jetways. Ground crews hand-lifted heavy luggage into the cargo holds in those days, long before motorized belt loaders were widely available. It has proved to be a constraint that engineers modernizing the 737 have had to work around ever since.

But by far the biggest issue was the engines. The new range of Airbus A320s had ultra-high bypass turbofan engines which, while much more efficient, were vast and heavier than previous designs. Adding this type of engine to the 737 was very challenging, since placing them in the existing location of prior engines made them perilously close to the ground. Since changes had to be minimal, the engines were placed far ahead of the wing leading edge to achieve ground clearance,

which had an alarming effect on the ability of the plane to fly.
This design decision meant the 737 MAX would tend to pitch up while accelerating or when the aircraft experienced a high angle of attack.

There is a big difference between a plane that is easier to fly, aided by software, and one that can't fly unless software is constantly working to keep the thing airborne. Boeing 737 MAX aircraft will remain aerodynamically unstable. They will still have a tendency for the nose to pitch during certain manoeuvres and in turn this could still lead to an increased risk of its engines stalling.

There are few shortcuts when it comes to profound transformation. Sticking new things on rarely works anywhere except at shareholder presentations and for a short period of time.

---

## CHAPTER SIX

# How to provoke and inspire change

*The ultimate aim of a business organization, an artist, an athlete or a stockbroker may be to explode in a dramatic frenzy of value creation during a short space of time, rather than to live forever.* KJELL NORDSTRÖM AND JONAS RIDDERSTRÅLE

How much of the built modern world appears to be the manifestation of rampant excitement about technology?

In 2021 around \$2 trillion was to be spent on digital transformation, and it had been over \$1 trillion for the last few years (Mlitz, 2021).

And what do we see for that? What companies do we accept as being champions of change? Look at the FTSE 100, Unilever, HSBC, Diageo, BP, Rio Tinto, Vodafone – do these feel like companies that have transformed? Take a look at the Nasdaq, or Dow Jones, or the CAC 40 in France, or the Fortune 500, and whether you look at the companies that have made more money than ever or those that are struggling year on year, it's hard to see real change. We need to consider why this is.

Strangely, most of the best pieces in management and business theory, both for today and the future, appear to have been written more than 20 years ago. The brilliant piece 'Why Good Companies Go Bad' by Donald Sull is a great example, where he talks at length about why companies fail. It is vital to understand the dynamics that he lays out, especially the idea of active inertia, the tendency to follow established patterns of behaviour within organizations and how often it's the innovation, the creativity and the fresh ideas that typically make success happen, then often create patterns that ensure a company will struggle to change again (Sull, 1999).

## Why is it especially hard for successful companies to change?

The four characteristics listed below explain why it is so difficult for companies to change.

### Strategic frames become blinders

Managers see the world through strategic frames; they are the mindsets, attitudes and ways of thinking in adapted routines. At first they are useful guidance but over time they calcify. They become a fixed outlook that resists change. They are a sense of how things are done, that we've always done it this way. Slowly but surely, especially in companies with strong cultural alignment and low diversity, strategic frames grow more rigid. Not only are existing ways entrenched but managers often force new and unexpected findings or information into existing schema or, worst still, ignore them altogether. It can be alarming how groups of people don't want to know the truth and want to merely be comforted.

### Processes harden into routines

Muscle memory in business is incredibly strong; the way that we do things evolves from suggestions for best practice to 'the ways things have always been done'. This doesn't mean that tried and tested processes are inherently wrong, but it is vital to always be open to a better way.

The routinization of processes can reduce the chance of radical breakthroughs.

## Values harden into dogmas

A company's values are the set of deeply held beliefs that unify and inspire its people. Values define how employees see both themselves and their employers. Values also provide the centripetal force that holds together a company's far-flung operations.

## Relationships become shackles

In order to succeed, every company must build strong relationships – with employees, customers, suppliers, lenders, and investors.

When conditions shift, however, companies often find that their relationships have turned into shackles, limiting their flexibility and making change hard. The need to maintain existing relationships with customers can hinder companies in developing new products or focusing on new markets.

## Why change?

I don't think it's simplistic to say there are two broad reasons for changing anything. You change either because you have to or because you want to. You change either out of fear or necessity or out of optimism, a need for pride, or excitement, or other such drivers.

For the last 10 years, and perhaps longer, the notion of change has mainly been driven by a narrative of fear. When analysts, shareholders or more likely consultants ask 'what is your blockchain strategy?', it seems to come from a sense of concern more than enthusiasm.

The primary battle in the world over the last five years has been between what we call legacy companies and what are phrased technology companies; both terms are lazy, vague and useless, but we've not found better expressions. Legacy companies by and large are companies with deep expertise, a track record of impressive revenue, and often year-on-year profit growth, which they typically return parts of to shareholders. Tech companies are typically thrusting insurgents built for the modern age with best-in-class technology at the core, but they often lack expertise in a particular category and generally have never made a profit. The idea that they are true 'technology companies' is clumsy. Airbnb isn't much more than a brilliant marketplace and website, Wayfair is just a furniture seller that doesn't operate stores, there is little proprietary tech behind Allbirds shoes or Emma mattresses or Cazoo car sales – the list goes on.

For many years the key question has been whether legacy company X in category Y can get good at technology before tech company Z gets good at category Y. For many years tech companies dominated the battles; Amazon got good at selling books before Borders got good at understanding technology. Netflix got good at entertainment delivery before Blockbuster could excel with new technology. Facebook got amazing at making money from advertising before media owners got good at technology.

But in the last few years things have been less sure. Uber may have dominated the taxi market but they have been unable to make any profits, something taxi operators did with ease. Airbnb may have more hotel rooms than any hotel chain, but profit continues to elude them, and hotels have hardly suffered any damage. Amazon seems less capable of making money from grocery or even most retail, while Carrefour, Tesco and Walmart all seem largely unscathed. Is Instacart bothering them? I think not.

We should probably ask why this is. Quite simply it's for two reasons.

## A move to less desirable categories

The early battles were held in places where the wins were easier, where there was a gap to serve. Books sales online make a lot of sense; they don't perish, they are easy and quite cheap to ship, and a large inventory is a huge advantage. DVD rental in expensive urban outlets is not an especially efficient idea, and there were clear advantages to newer business models. Increasingly the battlegrounds are in places where the benefits of being a new tech-driven company are less clear. Clothing has a wonderfully high margin, but the cost of advertising is huge and return rates cripple profitability. Neobanks seem like a great idea, but the customers with the desirable profiles likely need the trust provided by physical banks. Selling cars in person means you can sell complex profitable financial products and upsell people, taking advantage of them; selling online removes this ability. E-commerce is fast moving from demonstrably sensible categories like books, accessories and car parts to items like plants, furniture or even ice cream, where profit is simply very challenging.

## The power of tech disruption

When technology like fast, abundant connectivity combined with the rapid distribution of smartphones, cheaper computing and storage costs, and other advancements, a rapid new scope for innovation was created. Suddenly the potential for change was huge.

A plethora of early tech startups used this canvas of opportunity to challenge existing dominant players by simply doing things in ways that were much cheaper or much more efficient or just simply much better.

Skype allowed phone calls to be made over the internet, a clever hack to radically reduce the cost of telephony. Netflix was early to exploit the potential for streamed entertainment, and unleashed vast economic advantages of bypassing physical media. giffgaff decided it could radically reduce costs by letting a community of people, unpaid, become the customer support staff. Facebook similarly used its users to make the content people enjoyed, rather than paying to have it made. In many examples from Yelp to eBay to LinkedIn to WhatsApp, companies could enjoy very favourable economics as a result of exploiting new technology to greatly alter the costs of doing business. These are good examples of 'technology-based disruption' as coined by Clayton Christensen and mentioned earlier in this book.

The issue is that many of the modern technology companies that we celebrate are not benefitting from radically altered cost structures, or if they are very different to incumbents, they don't seem to be clearly better.

When Amazon delivers customers large electronics or shampoo or coffee makers, it may be avoiding the costs of retail outlets, salespeople and business rates, but it suffers new and different costs like packaging, delivery fees, and the cost of processing much higher return rates. A direct-to-consumer brand like Allbirds or Away luggage or Casper mattresses can indeed remove the markup by retailers, or rent, but their costs become hefty customer acquisition costs like advertising, customer support staff and, again, crippling costs of logistics in delivering to individuals. From Uber to Gorillaz to Airbnb to Spotify, at best many of these companies have very different fiscal dynamics and very different costs from incumbents, and with few exceptions, they rarely seem to have objectively more favourable economics.

The net result of all this is that we are wrong to assume that all the incumbent businesses are operating in an environment where threats are significant, urgent and clear. In many ways this explains the current environment where change is slow and superficial. We may like to think that the car rental business will be upended by dynamic thrusting startups, but it's not that likely, or won't happen at breathtaking pace. The hotel business will probably be OK with no change. The worlds of insurance, banking, charities, oil refineries, advertising agencies, furniture selling will probably be fine. These companies can probably continue to benchmark themselves against their typical competitors and they can improve as slowly as each other.

So if we don't have to innovate or transform from a place of fear, how do we bring change?

What if it was almost a moral imperative to use the power, influence and capabilities that we have to bring about the greatest change that we could make happen? What if we created a better future because we could? What if opportunity-based thinking drove us, not fear?

## What do you want to be proud of making happen?

That's quite an annoying question, but we may have to face the idea that pride can come from many places, but often job satisfaction, or even satisfaction in general, can come from seeing meaningful progress towards a consequential goal. AKA doing something that matters.

Modern life does such a good job of seeming to be overwhelming, chaotic, uncertain, changeable, that all too often we think of it as a storm to survive. At the same time, at the time of writing in late 2021, the world up until the Covid-19 pandemic had generally experienced about the most benign, positive, predictable and comfortable social, economic and political conditions we could ever hope for or imagine.

What could we do in our roles and life if we changed our approach from corporate survival to defining success as accomplishment or driving change? What if we sought to flourish, not hide? It is not that the world is without incredible changes to bring to life, or profound new technologies to explore.

There is a sense somehow that 'there is nothing new under the sun'. One can see the praise placed upon Europe's seventh-largest pet fitness tracker company, or see another influencer marketing content platform raise money, or a dating app for a new, smaller niche, or see yet another neobank or direct-to-consumer mattress company and assume we've got to grips with all that is new. But the real truth is that we're at the very early stages of rethinking the world.

Take a look around. We found a way to sell clothes online but never thought about why it is that so few clothes fit. What would the fashion industry look like in a world designed around the possibilities of technology, around new behaviours and changed parameters? What would cities look like if designed around people for the digital age, not cars? How could everything about homes and even home ownership change for the future? I don't just mean why does buying a home take a remarkably long period of time and involve incredible inefficiency, I mean how is it that we live in dwellings that have changed remarkably little since homes you will see in Greece, Turkey, Italy or Egypt from 3,000 BC?

How much of the modern world seems as good as it could be? How many industries seem excited about the advent of the internet, or 3D printing, or automation, or modular construction or augmented reality? How many websites make you amazed with the enthusiasm on display? How many products are designed brilliantly? From education to banking, to automobiles, to cities, to taxation policies, to voting, to charities, to welfare, to insurance, it seems there are so many places to reinvent key parts of the world around us.

## Opportunity-based thinking

*One of the very best questions in business is 'what if?'*

Nestlé would have been totally fine if it had never made Nespresso, now a billion-dollar business. It was not facing the looming threat of tech companies eating market share in coffee or food.

First Direct was a brilliant business idea from HSBC, but rather unnecessary. The world would have been fine without the Dyson vacuum cleaner, or Innocent smoothies. McDonald's didn't really need to rethink their stores to better serve customers in the digital age, because we all like Big Macs. Goldman Sachs is fine without Marcus, Facebook doesn't need to go into VR. Virgin doesn't need to go into space. Amazon doesn't need to make the Echo, Apple wasn't screwed without the iPad or Apple Watch. But this type of 'what if' thinking is where both profound growth and experiments that lead to enormous learning can come from.

## It is not indulgent to want to do more

Businesses, it seems, are primarily concerned about threats. They will change in accordance with the world around them. But, no one achieves first- or even second-mover advantage that way. Too much time and effort in business planning, strategy and investment is devoted to the T of SWOT – the Threats. The biggest prizes happen in the O part of the quadrant – the Opportunities.

Responsive strategies to developing threats have typically failed. British Airways seeking to defend against Ryanair with Go was too little too late, but the company would have struggled to make a business case to make it, until the threat was existentially scary, not least because it involved undermining their own offering. Large mattress chains would have never been able to sell online and direct without the rise of Casper looming over them, yet it's proactive steps to change or innovate before you have to that typically have allowed ideas to form in an optimistic environment and launch at the right time.

First Direct was launched in the UK by HSBC as a phone and internet-only bank in the 1990s. It worked because the proposition was simple. People were visiting branches less and less, and its rates were more attractive, even than HSBC's own. It is clearly an opportunity-based investment. HSBC realized that it could support a remote banking operation without cannibalizing its own retail business, because those customers attracted to First Direct would have gone elsewhere, rather than to HSBC.

It would be easy to consider Finn, launched in 2020 by JPMorgan Chase, as a carbon copy of First Direct. On paper, it looks the same: remote banking only with attractive interest rates. However, unlike First Direct, it bombed to the extent that JPMC has removed it from the market. The differentiator is that Finn was a threat-based investment; a reactive proposition launched at a time when fintech startups, with no legacy buildings or infrastructure, were pulling customers away from JPMC. Finn's market was much more competitive at its launch than that of First Direct. It also used many of JPMC's existing back-end systems, so opportunities to pull away from legacy technologies were squandered.

The number of new markets and chances to innovate – the Opportunities – remains near-infinite for businesses. For market innovation to be successful, customers need to understand a clear proposition including how their lives will be helped or enriched by it. First Direct worked because the proposition was clear. Finn didn't because its proposition was the same, at the time, as many others – and people don't have the bandwidth any more for 'just another brand' whose benefits are not quickly apparent. The waves of change are not just coming from technology in and of itself; the waves are coming from the customer.

### What used to be hard is now easy

Let's say in the year 2000 you had a dream to become the maker of a global candle business. Let's call it Mandles. It's candles scented like libraries or tar or tobacco. You'd first have to figure out how to procure thousands of candles or make them yourself, neither of which is easy. You'd then have to open candle stores around the world and employ hundreds of local staff – I'm getting uncomfortable already. You'd have to find ways to supply your candles to each market. Each store would need a fit-out, so that's an expensive design agency, and now you'd need to buy advertising to tell the world about your amazing Mandles. This sounds expensive. You'd probably need a media agency to buy ads, with a minimum spend of $100,000, and a creative agency to make the ads. You'd also need accountants to deal with your complex finances and definitely a lawyer or five to ensure you were doing the right thing in each market. You'd need someone to help you with payroll, another person in human resources, and how do you fund all this? We're looking at $1 million+ to open five stores around the world for a year to see if the idea works. And in 2000, who would fund this? Would a bank manager look at my track record of writing books and keynotes and advertising and think, yes, Tom is a candle-making specialist who has done well to hide his love of retail and operations for years – here is some money. I think not.

In 2021, if I have a dream of making candles I can do this. I use Upwork to find a brilliant advertising and packaging designer and mock-up packaging and some basic image-based ads for five scents of candle: Burnt Library, Smoking Tires, Roads After Rain, Teen Spirit and Oud Noir. This should cost me about $200. I open an advertising account on Instagram and Facebook, spend $300 on ads for each of these products that don't yet exist, that link to a landing page that another talented designer has made on Shopify for $200 and $20 per month. If it appears nobody in their right mind wants these candles, I quit, head to the pub and wallow in the regret of spending $720. If one scent takes off, I double down. I commission a seller on Alibaba to make these candles and drop ship them to each buyer from China, I up my ad spend, use the people who liked the idea as a lookalike audience, and a few clicks later can target similar folk. I can buy ads based on cost per acquisition and ensure I only pay for ads that convert.

I won't go on but the central idea is that everything we once found hard is easy.

**ACTION**

- To get your imagination going, and perhaps inspire you, think about some products or services you'd love to see exist.

- What need states do you have that seem remarkably underserved?

- What products do you wish were for sale?

- What apps would you make if you had access to the best talent in the world for free?

## Why has there been so little change?

I don't think we can really accept that we live in an era where large companies have transformed, or at least changed as much as they could have if powered by enormous enthusiasm, risk taking and a profound passion for new technology. Ask for examples of companies that have changed meaningfully and you will find the list is short. Microsoft have moved to selling subscriptions, not software, and impressively pivoted their culture to being more open and empathetic, Netflix moved from selling DVDs to being a vertically integrated entertainment behemoth. Oracle, Boeing, IBM and Dell are perhaps other examples, but the list is small and the depth of change still rather shallow. It's one thing for Boeing to move to selling service contracts on jet engines rather than just jet engines, it's another for Toyota to move from making cars to being a mobility company.

So how have we got to a place where we've a strong sense of chaos and complexity and defensiveness, and seemingly so little progress? I think there are three core reasons: we've misunderstood what digital disruption is and means, we've been let down by consultants who seek to reduce risk and maintain problems, and we've a system that disincentivizes companies to take risks. To be better placed to unleash profound positive change on the world around us, and I do hope this is what you want, we need to understand these further.

## Companies that are not incentivized to really change

We should ask why companies are behaving this way if we wish to change how they work.

Somewhat ironically, good management is what makes companies slowly fade: leaders hang on for long enough so they can retire comfortably. Companies are often run with one core strategy – survival – to maintain rigidity in the face of challenging conditions. Their departmental structures and processes embed this behaviour. Within this culture, compliant people are favoured, and management becomes a social construct more than an organizational one. Power comes from who owns the budgets and who's higher up the chain. Moving to more efficient, smaller teams often reduces the concentration of power. This means it is resisted by those holding such power, with emerging large-scale changes such as home/remote working further challenging the power base.

Consistent annual growth makes companies swell in size. Sure, they expand to new territories, they create new products and services, and their budgets and systems grow. Centralized corporate functions become staffed in a linear fashion to budgets, not to the workload required. A marketing department may have a sense that for every $10 million spent on advertising, a certain number of bums on seats are required. Departments exist to support themselves. The situation reminds me of those ultra-long flights between Singapore and New York, where a handful of passengers sit on what is basically a fuel tank. Most of the fuel is used to transport the other fuel.

In all honesty, many large companies don't really want to change. Publicly held companies in particular are especially difficult to pivot. Since the leadership team of all publicly traded companies are legally bound to maximize the returns of shareholders, they make management decisions based on these criteria. There are really only two kinds of company stock: stock for dividend and stock for growth. Businesses are powered by one type or the other.

## Dividend and growth stock

Investors know that McDonald's, Procter & Gamble, or any utility company are essentially dividend stocks. These companies offer a reliable source of income to shareholders each quarter by returning a large proportion of profits directly to shareholders. Nobody expects Coca-Cola to triple in price over a few months. They do, however, invest in it because it's unlikely to halve in price.

Growth stocks offer the exact opposite. From biotech companies to social media platforms, any company that can now credibly claim to be in 'the technology space' is able to tap into a supply of investors looking to make money, and can tolerate risk. And while we often think about all the tech companies that have performed incredibly well, we forget the less trendy ones which, for much of their post-IPO history, have languished. Others simply went bust.

The game plan for investing in growth stocks is to see a company use all of its income and cash reserves in order to grow – as quickly as possible. There are no expectations for the company to return any cash, and to do so implies a lack of confidence.

Investors often want a mixture of risk and different forms of return. They create a portfolio of high- to low-risk investments and long- to short-term bets. The market does not seem to have an enormous thirst to balance these dynamics within one company. People don't tend to look to companies like Unilever, Nestlé, Vodafone or American Airlines as a way to offer the prospect of medium growth with medium returns. They look to find a variety of companies that are optimized around one of these.

As such, the board and CEO are always defined by the nature of each investor's shareholding. A thrusting, young technology company will be tasked to drive growth as rapidly as possible, with risk being acceptable. For these companies, failing fast, pivoting and self-disruption are part of their journey.

But most of the companies that we tend to interact with each day are led by a team of people tasked with steering a steady path to maintaining profitability. For these, the name of the game is, at best, a steady survival. At worst, it's a slow decline.

P&G has done a superb job with creating new products, exploring new routes to market, and developing innovative marketing practices. However, such efforts are never about making massive changes to the bottom line, and they never involve significant capital investment. This is because such endeavours are not designed by the shareholders, and they are not defined by the requirements to hit revenue targets. Companies that find themselves in difficult markets, economic conditions, or facing renewed competitor threats turn to cutting budgets in order to maximize profit in the face of declining revenues. This is the very worst environment for digital transformation.

Given the combination of companies that don't really want to change but need to be seen as if they are, consultancies that are neither able nor want to bring about radical change, and a misunderstanding of the real threats and opportunities of 'digital disruption', what we get is innovation as distraction.

There is one big reason why large companies don't really undergo significant digital transformation: it's really hard.

Companies excel at doing the same thing over and over again – becoming ever more refined and expert. They are designed much like cargo ships: to cruise efficiently and relentlessly into a long, set course. However, it is their track record of success that becomes the most problematic element. Longstanding successes give organizations a clear, powerful and unified sense of their values, expertise, mission and strategy. They have a tightly defined formula for success, and that success has worked well for a long time.

When the marketplace changes, these strengths can become weaknesses. Firestone dominated the cross-ply tyre market for years. However, when Michelin introduced longer-lasting radial tyres, Firestone couldn't compete. It didn't help that radial tyres required more advanced manufacturing, and because they lasted twice as long, the lifetime value of a customer was potentially reduced.

Success often follows something of an s-curve. The pioneering, technology-led breakthrough of a new entrant leads to rapid success, which in turn offers a sense of superiority, confidence and a rigid devotion to formula. Such approaches can calcify from best practice and confidence to devotion to the status quo.

Our framework on how we see the world, offering structure to key strategic issues, can move from guiding principles to becoming a narrow worldview. Our assumptions become formalized as key performance indicators (KPIs), and bureaucratic ways to make decisions mean that companies can be blind to threats that develop, or they have opportunities that go unexplored. This often means that companies are unable to see others that seem to be substantially smaller or just materially different as offering up even the smallest of threats. Even as late as 2016, in an advertising pitch for a large German luxury auto maker, when I asked why Tesla was not in the competitive set for customers, I was laughed at. 'We don't sell cars for people whose concern is the environment' was the client's response.

---

**FAILURE CASE STUDY** Nokia

Nokia, thanks to the iPhone, is the poster child of disruption and the perils of failing to innovate. Having worked closely with them on their most advanced phones ever, the Nokia Nseries, for two years before and after the iPhone, I got insider access to a lot of the mistakes and dynamics at play. What Nokia got wrong was different from what people typically think. Nokia had been developing large, touchscreen devices, connected to the internet, with app-like programs for several years prior to the iPhone. It had an amazing reputation, boatloads of cash, amazing R&D teams making the best cameras, processors and other hardware around. What allowed Apple to succeed is vastly more complex than this, and only clear in hindsight, but it was linked to a lack of imagination and Nokia not taking its competition seriously. Having the best phones on the market, selling at amazing margins bringing in incredible profits for years didn't create complacency so much as a lack of focus and ambition. They saw the market as one they owned; customers were to be created by making the most advanced phones around. It never dawned on them that by approaching the market from a consumer perspective, and making something technically inferior but more delightful to use, like Apple, could entirely undermine their hardware and marketing prowess.

---

### ACTION

Test what you think are examples of these three approaches in an industry and perhaps discuss with a friend. The broad auto market is one example. Think of Zipcar, Turo, Uber, Avis, BMW ReachNow, Carvana, Silvercar, Book by Cadillac – which of these have digitized, digitalized and digitally transformed?

Consider an array of startups and establish the depth to which they've applied new technology to that category. Some names to kickstart you: Sonos, Casper, Instacart, Ocado, Allbirds, Blue Apron, Stitch Fix, Oculus, Monzo, Venmo, Lemonade insurance.

Pick any industry, perhaps your own, and visualize examples of each type of change.

## The three-step process to provoke

### 1) *Perform an inertia audit*

My time in consulting has revealed a great irony. The companies that we most often consider to be those best placed for the future are far more likely to ask for advice than those which seem almost beyond help. If one was logical then we would presume that it's companies like Sears, British Airways, Debenhams, Office Depot, Avon, Coty, Hertz or Jaguar Land Rover that would be asking for help. However, those that most need help seem least capable of asking for it, implementing recommendations, or investing in the company's future. The frog is boiling to death.

## 2) What could you do?

There are two ways to develop ideas and innovate.

Option one is around problems that exist in the world that you may be able to solve and have a right to.

Option two is around possibilities created by technology, as Tesla, DJI drones and Amazon Echo have exploited.

*The most obvious impetus for change comes from new technology but much comes from how the technology we've always had has changed people.*

The most obvious impetus for change comes from new technology but much comes from how the technology we've always had has changed people.

Technology has in many ways radically altered some aspects of how we live life. We seem to be more impulsive, we are happier to try new things, we are more open-minded to new ideas and new ways of doing things. Who would've thought that we would be happy getting in a stranger's car for a ride-sharing app? Who would've imagined that we would open up a bank account for a bank we cannot visit? Who would expect us to pick a hotel based on how easy it is to book it more than its physical attributes or price? We have less time, we seek easier choices, we want help making decisions, we are both busy but often bored. We may think the time on our phones is spent in a way that is so exhilarating that we are not bored, but most scrolling is rather mindless. In many ways the success of Instagram as a commerce platform will come from the fact that people are essentially looking for something to make them feel a bit alive and stimulated, which retail therapy satiates brilliantly.

We should look at the macro-economic environment. At this particular moment in time interest rates are very low and the cost of borrowing is remarkably cheap. Unemployment is remarkably low (all things considered) and the job market seems fairly robust. We are buying many things out of desire rather than necessity. And what we choose to buy now typically comes from the need to express who we are to other people or to make ourselves feel better. We lack meaning from many aspects of life, and products and experiences that we buy are typically there to fill the empty vessels that we are. Experiences in particular have become the new handbag, and social media sites have allowed us to broadcast our lives like never before. I just hope we remember to love them too.

Technology has changed the physics of business. The digital media of the internet has made globalization in particular easier than you could have ever imagined. Dropshipping allows even tiny retailers to sell to almost every country on the planet. Netflix was able to expand its reach to almost the entire planet without the requirement to employ new staff, instead just flipping a switch.

We now live in a time where access to capital seems especially easy. Entities seem to be almost tripping over themselves trying to offer money to lend. Savings rates are so low that anyone not putting their money to work feels like they are missing out. This is an amazing time to invest in yourself or your company.

We have access to almost every single piece of knowledge or wisdom that has ever existed. Anyone with a degree of curiosity and some time can almost train themselves to do anything. Knowledge has never been easier to acquire or more accessible. We can both connect with and access some of the best brains on the planet on demand. We can employ them to help in more flexible ways than ever.

Automation has reduced the cost of many elements of business, as have models to access what we need on demand. From artificial intelligence to image recognition to brilliant expert talent, we now have the ability to do things that were previously impossible to consider.

Normally a barrier to innovation and change, there are some forms of regulation sweeping the world that can inspire and allow new developments. The growth of cannabis products is a particular example of a sector going through extraordinary change due to regulations being altered; other examples include gambling, or planning laws in some parts of the world changing what sort of homes can be constructed, accessory dwelling units and tiny homes being key examples.

But the more obvious vectors in innovation come directly from new technology itself.

We should be keen to map out the meaning and implications of a variety of fast-improving and rapidly deployed advances in technologies like the following new combinations of tech. We are fast to celebrate pioneering companies enabled by ground-breaking, complex and novel technology, but forget that often it's a combination of fairly rudimentary technology in new ways. Ride-sharing apps like Lyft or Uber were only possible because of boring old technology like GPS and 3G connectivity. Similarly, apps like Sonder have leveraged the power of something as boring as an internet-connected smart lock to make something at the intersection of hotels and Airbnb – a gap in the market that makes commercial sense.

### 3) Create a business case for change

We've all stayed in hotels where things are slowly falling apart. However, if the owner tackles just one problem – the carpet, say – then it will end up drawing attention to the other problems. The owner might be wise to redecorate and re-equip all of the rooms.

If they do that to the rooms, then they should redecorate the lobby too. Oh, and install better Wi-Fi. And a gym. Once all that is done, repaint the outside. Now that the hotel is looking good, perhaps get a new website too. Maybe, instead of all that effort, building a new hotel might have been the better option.

What was the hotel's business case for change? Reviews might not be that great, but rather than spending $1 million, they could just lower the cost of the rooms and get by until things are really bad. Why take a risk?

However, there is no single day where the plan of what to do suddenly becomes clear. This is because the cost of doing nothing is impossible to ascertain. From Nokia not beating the iPhone, to Firestone losing to Michelin's radial tyres, the cost of not doing these things before someone else does simply cannot be estimated easily.

I've never worked in a company that was able to invest significant money or resources in radical change without a clear-cut business case, and rarely do processes like this allow the (hard to measure) cost of doing nothing to be a significant factor to include.

We've seen companies like the mobile operator O2 invent giffgaff, but only as a tiny passion project spurred on with great energy by Gav Thompson calling in favours, breaking rules with good intentions, until it became real enough and had enough momentum to be considered for relatively low investments. While car companies like Corvette or Dodge have a history of CEOs asking passionate employees to use spare parts lying around and spare time at weekends to bring to life brilliant new models that then become funded, there must be a better way, and creativity in business case development is a way ahead.

These questions and prompts should have your mind spinning, and you are now probably pondering on some profound thoughts. This chapter wasn't designed to start shaping ideas and approaches but merely to open the mind up to possibilities, warming muscles for change and hopefully bringing enthusiasm for what can be done. The goal was not to start shaping answers to questions, least of all starting to share the answers to key questions, but merely to warm up to change. The next chapter is about channelling this energy into useful directions where future opportunities can be understood and acted upon.

## CHAPTER SEVEN

# Creating a vision to transform

*Everyone takes the limits of his own vision for the limits of the world.* ARTHUR SCHOPENHAUER

If your entire company was erased from the planet, would anyone care? Would anyone notice? How many companies have you worked for that had a clearly defined sense of where they were going? Perhaps a 10-year plan? A clearly defined place in the world? A sense not just of competitors today but in the future? Do you know what your company will be about, how it will make money, what it will be proud of?

The expression 'How we spend our days is how we spend our lives' gives a nice little insight into how companies grow, progress and change over time. Companies are either defined proactively or reactively, and seemingly most are the latter.

How many ask questions like:

In the future, how will or can we make money? What are some of the new ways we might do that?

What can we absolutely not do?

What ways of making money will die out?
What can we reasonably predict will be the same?
What can we expect our current competition to do?
Where can we expect our future competition to come from?

We hear these days a lot about 'purpose-driven brands' and 'purpose marketing'; it's become a messy expression. About half of the time it's used, it's referring to a company being environmentally or socially responsible, a sense of greater good, and half the time it means 'does the company know why it exists?'.

The former is indeed admirable, and something to be covered by another book, but the latter is something far, far too important to forget. The reason why a company exists, its raison d'être, the rallying cry that binds staff, gives momentum and offers direction, is something both essential and typically missing. It's quite astonishing that so much energy and time can be orchestrated by an organization without a clear sense of where it's trying to get to in a broader or longer perspective than just end-of-year results.

## The pervasive lack of vision

It's puzzling to contemplate why so few people and so few entities actually have a very strong sense of where they are trying to get to. On a personal level, most people will say that their goal is to be happy or successful – others may say their goal is to earn six figures by age 30, or to get promoted next year. Few people seem to flesh out something less abstract than 'happiness' and more imaginative and profound than 'money next year' or a new car. I say this as someone without such a vision myself.

Given that companies are ostensibly made up entirely of people and are prone to display precisely the same traits, it's no surprise that most companies lack a guiding light, future scenario planning or even a mood board of success, or at least seem to.

Now, I'm sure some at a senior level will decry that their company has a vision. It will have mission statements online, forward-looking outlooks on the shared drive, a PR boilerplate talking about the path ahead, but does it really have a point of view? Is the statement more than a series of platitudes that remained after a well-attended brainstorm and consensus was reached?

Take a look at some of the most applauded mission and vision statements around (and please let's not get into a conversation about the difference, these are all the most widely shared declarations of ambition that exist in the world):

Amazon: 'Our vision is to be earth's most customer-centric company; to build a place where people can come to find and discover anything they might want to buy online' (Amazon, 2020).

IKEA: 'To create a better everyday life for the many people' (IKEA, 2021).

Samsung: 'Inspire the world, create the future' (Samsung, 2018).

Southwest Airlines: 'To become the world's most loved, most flown and most profitable airline' (Southwest Airlines, 2020).

Walgreens: 'To be America's most loved pharmacy-led health, well-being and beauty company' (Walgreens, 2021).

---

**ACTION**

Pick a company you admire but think is lost, one you find interesting and unusual – what do you think the 10-year vision should be? What role could they play in your life? What role could they obviously not?

---

None of these is an especially useful, compelling, precise, inspirational or ambitious statement about the future. Some seem to limit growth by being over-specific. Amazon wanting to 'help people find and discover anything they might want to buy online' already seems counter to their plans in healthcare or even video online. Some are so vague as to be rather useless, but sound nice. Some seem to limit imagination by being overprescriptive.

Do you feel these companies have a strong sense of where they are going? Could you tell me a product or service these statements would help inspire? Or if they would help shape an acquisition strategy? Do you get a strong sense of the threats, opportunities, weaknesses, trends, changes in the geopolitics of the world, changes in behaviours or regulations that lie ahead? How many work around the possibilities of new tech, the adoption of it, or changed consumer understanding?

While it's the case that mission statements are designed to be pithy, short declarations of intent, I'm unaware of these companies having more lengthy, prescriptive, inspiring copy behind the scenes. I'm not aware of the existence of any corporate tool or templates for a bold, clear, empowering, future-focused, ambitious rallying cry. While perhaps they exist in private, we see little proof that these companies are following a well-crafted roadmap to the future in the decisions they make. When plans are shared in public like Facebook's 10-year plan at F8 in 2016, it seems like a list of random technologies like drones, satellites, lasers, along with AI and VR, while saying: 'We are building the technology to give anyone the power to share anything they want with anyone else.' Which doesn't add much illumination, and jars against their investments in making content, or acquiring customer relationship management (CRM) companies.

We think the future is too unknowable to project and plan how we make money or what we should make or what companies to acquire, so most modern business is really defined by the here and now. Targets move from ambitious, perhaps vague and in the future, to KPIs that are very specific, manageable, day to day, and, well, a measurement of proxies, mere indicators of the pulse of the organization but not where it is going. Instead of a lofty vision, we're held to account by employee retention ratios, net promoter scores, readership, and other things less likely to mean your role is aligned to a future ambition that matters. We become guided by proxies, not passion.

It sometimes seems companies become defined by their history, and a vision is a reactive attempt to best retrospectively merchandise great decisions. A lot of companies appear to be the result of billions of tiny everyday decisions with no overriding goal in mind. I think few of the agencies that I've worked for ever had any sense of a future path other than just whatever it took today and next month to 'be OK'. Few decisions ever seem to be made with respect to some grand plan.

Many tech companies seem guided less by a strong sense of future role and more as the result of thousands of 'test and learns', lots of 'failing fast' and billions of A-B tests. Does anyone think that the Amazon homepage is clearly the best possible homepage Amazon could ever make or is it just an optimization of every optimization they've ever tried? Tech companies often seem to never really have a particularly strong sense of long-term direction; we may marvel at the degree to which they can pivot so easily and quickly, but typically forget it's because they set out in a direction without as much thought as one would hope. A test and learn approach is smart, but even smarter is relishing the notion of deep thought before restless execution.

*A test and learn approach is smart, but even smarter is relishing the notion of deep thought before restless execution.*

A third category seems to be companies guided by a sense of following best practice, current management orthodoxy and some little trends; a whole array of companies seems to create new copycat products or make acquisitions based on what their competition is doing.

## The need for a future vision

For many companies the vision is a clear, concise statement to outline beliefs and ideologies. Something used as a rallying cry, and that is known and understood by all members of the organization. This is the archetypal vision that we see above.

I think vision needs to be articulated more clearly, and should include milestones, a measurable goal. There should be documents that describe in a compelling way why the company exists, who its customers are, how it makes money, what role it has in the world, who it employs, and what assets and intellectual property (IP) it has.

A clear vision like this provides inspiration but clarity; decisions become easy as a destination is clear. Typically, it involves 'ownership' of a tightly defined, but expansive, inspiring, logical and ambitious remit.

A clear vision should aid the development of the structure of your company, help inspire, define and shape the products and services you make and the underlying business model beneath them. It will give clarity on the talent you need to hire, the assets you need to invest in, the R&D you need to undertake. It can inform the companies to acquire, the investors to take money from and the people on your board.

But so much more than this, the beauty of a clear vision is that it allows the confidence to say no to 99 per cent of things. Modern life is one of abundance, and the skill is knowing what not to read, who not to talk to, what meeting to skip, what technology to ignore. Most companies' vision is an exercise, in a world where anything is possible, in saying no to many things many thought sensible. It's useful here to contrast Apple and Amazon. Amazon seems to have a business development approach of just saying yes to everything and seeing what happens. Apple seems to be so focused on saying no to almost everything that it can be rather disappointing as a shareholder, consumer or fan to see them ignore several key areas they could dominate if they wanted to, from electronics to services to software.

## A checklist for your vision

Before starting to create your vision, three questions, which are there to guide ideas, not form them, could be pondered.

## How futuristic should this vision be?

Depending on your industry, the future may be wildly chaotic or oddly predictable and this should help shape the date in time for which your vision is set. It's likely the baked bean or wine or prescription drug development market is unlikely to be wildly different in 15 years, but the automotive industry or software industry likely will be.

Your ability to make changes fast, a function of size, culture and money, can also help set a benchmark for the future that gives you long enough to make meaningful change and be enough time to have great ambition.

I would suggest that for most companies, a vision for less than three years ahead isn't likely to be a bold vision that can rally the masses, it's likely to be a strategy or tactic to help create marginal improvement. Similarly, a future vision for 30 years' time is likely to start debates that distract from focus. Do you want discussions about whether we live on Mars, about nano-bots or flying cars, to derail your thinking? The further ahead the vision is, the harder it is to get buy-in for action now, and the more prone it is to being wrong.

Future visions are likely best when set for between five and twelve years away.

## How restrictive should it be?

Is it tight enough to be inspiring, loose enough to be interesting?

'Give me the freedom of a tight brief' is the copywriter's mantra, but useful for vision setting. A vision should exist to help answer many questions and inform conversations about structure, talent, business model, investments, and so much more. The way to resolve the requirement for specificity and room is to do two things: be clear, and be adaptable. Clarity of vision and being prone to demonstrative examples are great ways to flesh out something vague but with guardrails. Accepting that things change, but are variations on a plan, is a great way to build in the way companies need to adapt. It seems sensible that a bank may want to leverage the trust it has to become the 'vault' of personal data; an office provider may want to move from being a renter of space to a company that helps workforces be productive. It's useful to have a notion of the sorts of questions your vision needs to answer over time, and ensure its clarity can enable that.

### Is this the right ambition level?

It's tempting in all corporate settings to demonstrate passion, enthusiasm, belief and ambition by being wildly unrealistic. Especially in the United States, people would rather work with someone who thinks their company is going to take over the world, than capture decent market share in the locality. Being too ambitious leads to ridicule and means every element of the vision loses any credibility and attracts scorn, while a vision that is too easily within reach will ensure atrophy takes place and will provide zero forward momentum, advertising a lack of drive across the company and to stakeholders.

Ambition should be based on interpolating current progress and current dreams into the future. It should be carefully assessed relative to current trends, market dynamics and likely changes in the future as well as competitor activity. To some extent, ambition need not be precise. It's better to have a clear, credible direction in mind, but which ends up being too far away to reach, than to have something that didn't drive action. To this end, ambition should be less of an input and more of a sense check at the end, to ensure people didn't go wild.

With the questions and parameters in mind, we can next start to embark on the journey to create a vision. If it's now easier than ever to shift to anything, to make money in new ways, to grow faster in new categories or to increase your valuation by being a tech company, then what should your company do or be?

There is a nine-step process for this.

## Nine steps for a vision

### Step 1: What are you really about?

Every company is rooted in a core competency. For years any organization or entity has rallied around a certain value that they offer consumers, that they either excel in doing or do better than others. Oil companies are great at finding and extracting oil. Luxury brands are great at creating desire for well-crafted goods. Hotels are amazing at hospitality. They will have created processes, employed talent and invested in assets with these specific forms of value creation in mind. The first step in this process is to simply look at the key skillsets and attributes that you have. What knowledge, expertise, culture do you have at your disposal, especially relative to other companies? This could be anything – incredibly deep consumer understanding, strong sales skills, brilliant technical staff. A company like British American Tobacco likely has an enormous pedigree and depth of knowledge when it comes to procuring and processing tobacco, but likely none of the skills in software, electronic engineering, product development needed to create something like an e-cigarette. A car company like Honda has incredible experience in hydrogen cars, but little when it comes to the skills needed to build out a charging network like Tesla. BP may thrive in the world of oil supply, but is it in the best place to move into opening EV charging networks or to move into green energy?

Knowing the centre of what you do best is a vital first step, and doing so in relation to your current and future competitors is key. The act of building a vision isn't purely about interpolating this broad capability into the future, or to greater heights, but knowing what you do best is a good way to start. But again, don't use this as a limitation, just context.

### Step 2: What sort of company should you seek to be?

There is a widespread belief that there are only really four types of company in the world: asset builders, service providers, technology creators and network orchestrators.

Asset builders are companies that make, market, distribute and sell physical products. Service providers train and recruit skilled people to sell a service they offer. More recently there have been technology creators, people who develop and protect intellectual capital to develop and sell largely intangible or high-margin products. And most recently we've seen the rise of network orchestrators. These are marketplaces or social networks or other networks created to produce, market and sell goods, services or information.

While I find these descriptions rather baffling, and would struggle to place most businesses in them satisfactorily, they do help frame the way companies HAVE been described, built and operated. Realistically most telcos do operate more like asset owners than service providers; a car-sharing app like Turo is absolutely a network orchestrator while Hertz is an asset builder.

The digital world allows companies to move across these lines. Companies with subject matter expertise, a trusted brand, relationships, distribution and/or other key assets or attributes can now more easily than ever before shift from making products to services, from hardware to software, from things to experiences. Consider companies like Disney, which operates theme parks and cruises, makes films and entertainment, operates large retail outlets and has a huge licensing business, all as a mutually supportive flywheel. Nike has slowly moved out from being a fashion label that makes sports clothing for wholesalers to sell on, to being a maker of fitness apps, devices like NikePlus, as well as now moving to become a retailer that sells directly online and off. Nestlé's Nespresso turned a coffee maker into effectively a subscription service.

More recently we've seen a number of companies start to cross traditional boundaries.

Peloton is a hardware company selling spinning bikes with excellent software but also a media and content creation business. It's this that inspired sports clothing maker Lululemon to buy Mirror (a home gym equipment maker) for $500 million in 2020 (Gray and Kruppa, 2020).

In 2004, Prudential (an insurance company) launched PruHealth, a technology platform that offered lifestyle benefits like gym access and reduced health insurance costs for living a healthier life. IKEA has now acquired a range of companies including a 49 per cent stake in a bank, an augmented reality company to aid in visualizing furniture, and TaskRabbit, an app to find people to undertake everyday tasks for you.

Based on these different business models and your core competence, what appears to be the best type of company to be? It is certainly easier to get higher valuations if you are in some sectors compared to others but there are also challenges in doing that.

## Step 3: Assess your current situation more broadly

Every company has a variety of intangible and tangible assets. The central starting point should be to assess the makeup of a company, to get a feeling for what kind of platform you are to launch off.

In addition to core competence, look at:

REPUTATION AND BRAND VALUE

Brands and other elements of reputation like trust are incredibly hard, expensive and slow to build. Well-defined brands typically help outline sensible areas for exploration.

What does your brand allow you to do easily, vs hinder you? Some industries like healthcare or banking require enormous trust, some sectors need fashion credibility. It's quite easy to see that Facebook, which has trust issues, could not be a bank. IKEA could do housing quite easily but would not feel right making cars. Nike could own gyms and perhaps health insurance but could likely not become a healthcare provider.

American Express was first set up as a rival to the American Postal Service shuttling post between the east and west coasts – hence the name – but banks proved to be the firm's best customers, so American Express established its own money-ordering service in 1882. Something made much easier by trust.

## RELATIONSHIPS AND PARTNERS

P&G has worked hard to gain distribution, sales execs with amazing relationships with retailers and complex commercial agreements, something worth an incredible amount of money and not easily replicated by others. You may have commitments to franchise owners or a complex political structure that doesn't enable radical change. Do an audit of all of the relationships that matter.

## ASSETS

From factories that make OLED screens to patents, to car dealerships, to land containing gold, it's vital to assess the assets you have in place. They could be employees, factories, huge amounts of customer data and existing customers, and understanding this will instinctively guide you to what your company could realistically move to or build upon. Note that quite often assets become barriers to change. If you own a plant making photographic paper, moving to digital imaging is troublesome. If you have thousands of unionized workers, moving to a nimbler organization is tricky. A company that has invested billions in buying cruise ships can't easily shift to online experiences without appearing to lose face or show a lack of faith in the company leadership.

## Step 4: Look at new technologies and new dynamics in the business world

The implications of new technology are notoriously difficult to predict, especially the timing of the changes and how technologies will combine with other tools to bring about enormous changes in the world. Depending on the sector, it's worth mapping out developments like artificial intelligence, robotics and automation, improved batteries, improvements in LED lights, 5G, graphene, CRISPR, modular construction and a whole array of other changes to see how that inspires and shapes your discussion.

Investigate which of these technologies can have a transform-ative impact on your sector. You can also look at the ones that could be detrimental to the space that you wish to go into.

**ACTION**

Innovation and transformation are an exercise in focus.
What technologies or movements in technology can you reasonably ignore? What technology do you need to learn more about to be able to decide?

## Step 5: Look at new economics, demographics and regulatory or political influences

We need to outline the broader environment in which our vision is to exist. It's typical to fall back on a tried and tested technique like PESTLE – Political, Economic, Social, Technological, Legal and Environmental changes.

Now we've elevated technology to do it first and in its own section, but we also probably need a more specific and imagina-tive approach towards considering these variables.

Broadly speaking, when people are undertaking processes like this, they tend to rely on things that make them seem clever and are objectively true; it's better to look at these in more enlight-ened and imaginative ways.

When looking at the economy, for example, it's easy to look at interest rates, but what may matter more is borrowing rates, or lending criteria. When looking at the environment, it may be less about climate and environmental policies, and more about people's attitudes to consumption in an era of growing concern about climate change.

Some of the things that I find are often helpful are changes like urbanization. In living memory the world has only become more urbanized; it's one of the longest-lasting trends one could imagine, as money is hard to make from the land. But we should have an open mind to the idea that technology like self-driving cars and video calling combined with the post-pandemic era may radically change our attitudes towards where we live. We may not see a huge leap in the numbers of people moving to the countryside but the kinds of people who go there may be particularly instrumental.

We should be thinking a lot about wealth distribution and to be quite frank we should be planning around a world that has a large number of people with almost indescribable wealth, and a somewhat vanishing middle class in many parts of the world. We should also be aware that while relative wealth may broaden, absolutely wealth may increase. To be in the lowest 10 per cent of wealth in the year 2020 is a very different lifestyle from that of 1980, let alone 1880.

From climate change to taxation to globalization to attitudes to privacy or working hours, to our attitude towards work, there is a lot to consider.

## Step 6: Look at new dynamics and behaviours in the consumer landscape

### CHANGED BEHAVIOURS
How has technology changed the way that people behave? One example, Airbnb is an interesting idea that would have failed if the founders had listened to most people; the notion that you would pay money to stay in a stranger's house is something rather counterintuitive to this moment in time. Yet the internet has changed our sense of trust, and armed with decent reviews and a belief that Airbnb will do some host checking, we're seemingly happy to do the previously unexpected. The internet means people can now be more spontaneous – HotelTonight built on this idea. E-commerce makes shopping malls more for fun than buying, with department stores finding out they don't need to exist.

## Step 7: Look at emerging and threatening competitors

Traditionally our mindset towards competitors has been dominated by the past and our lack of imagination. Not long ago, Porsche were focused on their competitor set of Audi, BMW and Mercedes-Benz. For them the idea that Tesla could ever be a threat was beyond their imagination because Tesla was a car for people who care about the environment.

Companies tend to consider that other companies most like them are the threats – department stores benchmark themselves against other department stores, luxury clothing companies look at other luxury clothing companies, large banks see other large banks, you get the idea.

*The very worst place to really assess your competition is from within that industry.*

But people don't make decisions this way. Luxury fashion is in some ways about expression but also status and may compete with art, with expensive travel, with fine dining. We need to have a view of looking more widely at what can compete for our wallets, our time, our brain space.

We should also be aware that companies can grow extremely quickly. Nokia never once considered Apple a competitor until it was too late, Yahoo never thought about Google. We tend to want to use competitor analysis as a way to look better by comparison to companies that frame us well.

But more than anything else, the most threatening dynamic in the modern marketplace is that of asymmetrical competitors. Banks see themselves as being defined very tightly by a group of competitors that are following the same regulations and are based on the same principles. Credit card processors like Mastercard or Visa would see only American Express as in the 'same market'. Consumers have absolutely no interest whatsoever in how companies work, they just have things they need to do.

For most people today HSBC, Barclays, Monzo, Mastercard, Apple Pay, Venmo, PayPal, Klarna, or Alipay are all pretty much the same thing to them – they are things you can use to spend money. Yes, banks can do more, but digital wallets and banks in particular are closer than anyone in that industry would ever imagine, and that's the tricky thing, the very worst place to really assess your competition is from within that industry.

## Step 8: Assumptions

I've mentioned before in this book the idea that disruption is really about challenging assumed constraints. This is a process where you ensure either rules holding you back, or rules you are planning your future state around, are indeed real and true.

What assumptions have your company and its competitors made? Starbucks assumed that people will pay more for coffee; Dyson, that people will spend $600 on a vacuum; Ryanair, that you can create demand to fly to strange places if you are cheap enough, like stag dos in Tallin.

These could be assumptions about the rate of progress in technology, about the economic environment, about trends in behaviours, about your competitors. Develop a sensible, smart approach to testing these criteria, using some as tensions to ideate around. Ask questions. What if we could move bank accounts in one click? What if open API architecture allowed this to happen? What if packaging got better and people could get this by mail? What if people were happy to place trust in an online-only business? What if people didn't want choice, they wanted ease? The list goes on.

**ACTION**

One day simply take note of all the even slightly questionable interesting, powerful assumptions made in meetings you attend. Ones that, if they turned out to be untrue, could unlock huge potential.

It's typically quite an eye-opening experience. With this framework in place, we can brainstorm and form ideas around this principle.

### Step 9: Carve out a role

When Harvard marketing professor Theodore Levitt said to his students, 'People don't want to buy a quarter-inch drill. They want a quarter-inch hole', we started to think about products and marketing in new ways (Christensen et al, 2005). Clayton Christensen famously took this further with his 'jobs to be done' framework (Christensen et al, 2016). The idea here was that we are not so much in the business of selling items, drills, milkshakes or new watches, but are actually trying to accomplish something bolder and more ambitious.

Airbnb is a great example, once 'a roof over your head' regardless of how it was delivered, with first an 'Air mattress and Bed And Breakfast' and later, more proper beds and fewer breakfasts. The platform can now grow in two very interesting horizontal directions: it can stand for humanity and the idea of 'people helping people', which allows it to run tours (as it has started to do); but it also offers potential expansion into anything about people that requires trust, such as casual jobs, food preparation, ride shares. The business can be propelled in any direction that requires a reputation online and the codification of trust.

And it could also move vertically. It could branch out into the 'housing' arena, building (or leasing out its name to) liveable hotels, friendly-feeling apartments, murphy beds, and interior design. Airbnb has the potential to stand for anything in the horizontal or vertical. That's quite something.

Thinking about the role your business plays in people's lives is a big way to grow. The roles of many incumbents are under threat and this is the core issue.

When we think of it this way, life becomes exciting for many. Gyms are not places you pay money to each month in order to access their space and machines; they become holistic lifestyle organizations that can help you attain any goal.

Banks can stand for being the gateway to spending, saving, all the bills we pay. They can go from being places to trust with our savings, to being the guardians and advisors on financial health.

Do you want to be in the office provision business or in the industry of creating productive teams?

Mobile operators around the world are terrified about being 'dumb pipes'. How can they leverage the relationship they have with all of us and our billing details, and become owners of content, managers of mobile payments, advisors in our relationship with data and news?

The role you wish to fulfil in a consumer's life becomes the focal point of your vision. Perhaps you want to move from a shoe brand to a lifestyle partner in athleticism; perhaps you make Botox but you want to make a consumer-centric tech business about improving your beauty; perhaps you once made amazing loudspeakers but want to be about audio experiences in the world. It should be a territory that is ownable, exciting, empowering, profitable and you have the means to try to dominate.

## ACTION

We tend to see the world as we are. Imagine if someone from a totally different sector was running this exercise for you – how would someone from fashion carve out a role? How would someone from entertainment or electronics or government see the value you bring and combine that with their typical approach?

Alternatively, what would Steve Jobs or Richard Branson or Warren Buffett or Jeff Bezos or Elon Musk or anyone else you know about do?

## A key thing to remember is to pick the right attitude

It's vital to establish how 'high' your company or brand can go up a ladder of benefits in consumers' lives and not lose relevance or credibility, or stretch your current core competencies and expertise too far.

A company making subversive direct-to-consumer men's socks shouldn't find it hard to become a seller of women's subversive socks, or even all socks to all people, and perhaps even underwear or all intimate garments, but it's unlikely to have the best base to become a company that dominates 'fitness' or 'health' or even a lifestyle brand that can sell sofas.

An online mattress seller like Casper or Emma will quickly see how they can sell both online and offline, can extend new products to pillows, throws, beds, and become a smaller part of a bigger market like the 'world of sleep' or 'home furnishings'. A very ambitious leader may claim Casper can become a brand or company that is really selling 'serenity' or 'happiness', but such high altitudes can quickly lead to incredulity and massive loss of focus. If you're selling cushions and mattresses, it's a pretty big leap of faith to expect to sell 'happiness'; does that mean retreats, coaching, therapy, pharmaceutical drugs?

There is a careful balancing act. 'Peloton uses technology and design to connect the world through fitness, empowering people to be the best version of themselves anywhere, anytime' is perhaps a little of a stretch, but a lot more inspiring and full of potential than just being the maker of an expensive bike.

---

**FAILURE CASE STUDY**   WeWork

WeWork quickly attracted scorn when trying to change its name to 'We' and positioning itself as a community company with a mission to 'elevate the world's consciousness'. The We company sought to be 'a network for augmenting humans' which gave it permission to make schools called 'WeGrow', places to live called 'WeLive', and even cities for the future called 'WeCity' – to 'build a world where no one feels alone'. It seemed to do a good job of defending a preposterous valuation compared with other office rental companies, but it also led to a massive loss of confidence, as early attempts to sell short-term apartment leases and schools seemed disastrous and distracting.

---

Expand and articulate this vision, define it more closely, plan out some typical consumers – how they buy it, when they buy it. Why do they choose you over other people? Who else will be in this space? Is the space something you have the right to play in? Stress the vision to make it tight, empowering and compelling. And now for the last step.


## Create an indicative roadmap

It would be wildly difficult to do any form of navigation without a sense of some points on the way. Not least because any suffi-ciently faraway destination would appear to be overwhelming. Companies should not develop tight, constraining roadmaps as to do so would be impossible and restrictive, but an outline sense of milestones and gates to pass through will aid with two things.

Roadmaps give immediate direction and focus. A 15-year plan may have one-, five- and ten-year destinations to guide the way, and it is the presence of these checkpoints that allows people to coherently form more realistic plans for now.

They offer a sense check on the vision, helping ensure it's sufficiently ambitious, defined and, well, sensible. If your 15-year plan to move from selling nutritional smoothies to ingested healthcare nanorobots requires you to patent a new type of robot in a year, you know you're on the wrong track.

These roadmap checkpoints should be frequent enough to be helpful and reassuring, not limiting, and include key metrics to assess and evaluate progress against. Clear goals are essential in life and they immediately inspire and provoke plans.

With a well-defined vision in mind, key questions answered about ambition levels, timescales, risk tolerance and more, and ideally a loose roadmap to act as a progress and direction check, we can now start to formulate what your company should look like and then how to get there. This is a focus on operations, the process, structure, technology and people within your new organization.

The next chapter will address the first three and Chapter 9, the people and culture.

## CHAPTER EIGHT

# Operations for the digital age

*You never change things by fighting the existing reality.
To change something, build a new model that makes the
existing model obsolete.* ELKE HACKL

The very core question behind this book has always been, what would your company look like if you built it today and how do you build what you should have? Has technology changed how you sell things, or what you make? Or how you make it? How has it changed how we work? What our roles are? Where and when we work? What does new technology mean for the structure of our companies, their policies, processes and technologies they use? All good questions I attempt to address in this chapter.

In the 20 years I worked within companies, reorganizations were seemingly never-ending. If we were not about to reorganize, it was because we just had. In the last 10 years I never saw our company's organizational chart – I think it was too hard to keep up to date. In the rare moments we were not reorganizing, our clients were. I'm not saying it didn't work, but I can't remember any real sense of progress. The reason is that it's incredibly hard. Trying to be fast but deliberate, trying to enable complex, rich human communications but not be slow and bureaucratic, trying to manage quality and accountability but also letting people be free. It's impossible.

What can be done properly is to explain how we got here.

## How did we get here?

The vast majority of successful but traditional companies have been constructed around principles, assumptions, limitations and best practice of the past.

For the first large companies ever to have existed, and the army before that, management of assets was the name of the game. In the mid-19th century, Ford, Carnegie, Vanderbilt and Rockefeller powered corporations by devising methods for managing assets efficiently. They formed bureaucratic systems and procedures designed to maintain control and consistency within an organization. Bureaucracy is a term that has recently become pejorative, but at its heart, it's a system of order and record keeping that includes division of labour, management, hierarchies and coordination. It's a system known for formality, logic, rationality and rules, not relationship; process, not judgement. It's binary.

At this time, quality and consistency of bureaucracy would be a key competitive advantage. Companies could keep accurate records, organize the flow of information, and cut down on waste through more efficient use of resources. Companies became (and remain) inward-looking, with few staff employed to look into the future or focus on consumers; instead there was a maniacal focus on improvement of the machine, not the product.

Over time, successful companies have generally become ever larger, as measured by revenues and profitability but also by assets owned and staff employed. Companies facing such circumstances became both complex and deep, with layer upon layer of management.

We forget this now, but before email it was expensive and slow for one person to send a message to more than 10 people. In a pre-digital age it was mathematically impossible for companies to be able to effectively monitor and talk to (and perhaps listen to) 5,000 people without X levels of management.

In the past, work revolved around being in the same place as others and at the same time. Factories operated with people like cogs. The working day is eight hours not because it's the best way to add value but because it allowed three shifts of eight hours a day in a relentless, ongoing, repetitive 24-hour day:

- **Needs and possibilities have changed**
  The possibilities of technology do alter the assumptions and frameworks that we've constructed our companies around.
- **A focus on customers**
  Peter Drucker once wisely wrote that 'the purpose of business is to create a customer' (Drucker, 1954); what always amazes me is how few companies seem to think, let alone operate this way. We need to remember who is boss, and it's the customer.
- **A focus on ideas**
  If commands of control in the past were driven first by power and order and then by knowledge, it's now insights and ideas that become the lifeblood of growth. Orienting yourself to maximize the quality and quantity of ideas generated demands very different systems.
- **Talent**
  Careers were once about climbing a corporate ladder, but are now increasingly about providing skills, relationships and financing for people to do their own thing. Keeping the right kind of culture and values alive in your company comes from having an empowered and committed workforce.

- **Influence**
  Flatter management structures allow for more collaboration and therefore necessitate more of a democratic approach.
- **Outcomes**
  Rather than measure productivity in hourly output, focus on the real value your workers bring from enhanced relationships, innovation and customer satisfaction.

## So how do you build the future operations of your company?

### Step 1: Remind yourself of the evolved qualities for your sector

Organizational design should start with corporate self-reflection: how will you make a difference for your clients, employees and investors? What will set you apart from others, now and in the future? What differentiating capabilities will allow you to deliver your value proposition over the next three to ten years? What is your sense of purpose?

In order to best do this, remind yourself of the vision you have for the future, and focus on the core elements you need to deliver against this vision. It's likely about what core competency you need, but it may also include key knowledge, key intellectual property, key experiences, or products.

### Step 2: Establish your broad approach to digital transformation

As we have discussed before, there are three broad strategies for transformation:

1 We can digitalize, by applying technology to the outermost layers and hoping the changes slowly permeate through the company.

2 We can digitally transform by using technology at the core and rethinking the entire company's mission, business model, processes and structure with technology cascading outwards.

3 Or we can digitally create. We cannot give up on our existing entity, but accept that change is harder than creation and place measured bets of money, resource and energy on developing new entities that could either become our future or in other ways aid it.

The most significant criterion that will influence your strategy is the vision you have developed in the previous chapter. What is the core value you add or make, and what skills and structure do you need to get there? Secondly, an audit of your current assets, capabilities, structure, knowledge, data and reputation will ascertain the degree and type of change required.

If you are an asset management firm, owning and operating shopping malls across the world, and you wish to become a Shopify-like platform that powers online retail around the world, it's likely that what you currently have and do is (with exceptions) not the best starting point, and digital creation is a great strategy.

If you are a chain of sportswear retailers, with a brilliant reputation for wonderful customer service, brilliant frontline staff, great relationships with sporting manufacturers and owned stores in great locations but you want to become more of a 'community hub for sports and healthy lifestyles', then you can probably add on a few people to your existing teams, use some nice new event-planning software, improve your websites, improve your content marketing, add some advanced CRM, and generally improve by sprinkling a little technology around the edge.

## A MINDSET TO VISUALIZE DIGITAL TRANSFORMATION

The slow demise of some companies feels a bit like ageing. Over the years we accumulate knowledge, habits, memories, structures, baggage and defects. We become jaded, we don't like risk, and we don't learn so fast. We start to dislike and then fear change as we get older and the truth is we've less and less energy and see less reason to alter our lives. We get more closed-minded, we seek to preserve, not grow. We've stopped looking for a rapid career ascent, and are instead seeking a dignified, relaxing, predictable, and ideally prosperous glide path to comfort.

When faced with the reality of our ageing bodies, we seemingly face a few options.

We can turn to surgery. From Botox to facelifts, to nips, tucks and augmentation, we can almost immediately, with known and manageable investment and little risk, create the illusion of youth. We can distract ourselves and those who see us from the cracks that lay beneath. Perhaps if we buy sports cars, hang around younger people, buy more fashionable clothes, we can try to convince ourselves we're young.

Or we can have therapy and make lifestyle changes. We can get better at seeing change in context and come to terms with our demise and seek to find the best ways to focus on what matters. This can be deeper, slower, and non-invasive change. With a better diet and some yoga we can perhaps live a little longer, but we are mainly focusing on how we can feel better about our impending tragic but inevitable expiration.

But the truth is, regardless of nips and tucks, downward dogs and therapists' couches, we will die. If we truly, really want our spirit to live on, if we really believe in what we offer and seek to find a sustainable way to ensure the essence of us remains, we have kids.

Kids ensure that our meaning and the purpose and value that we represent are enduring and worthwhile. Having kids is the natural order of the universe, not a modern invention to reduce ageing.

Superficial 'innovation' can be the cosmetic surgery of the modern age. Something that offers zero chance of increasing longevity, but something to distract the market, something that looks compelling and arresting, is rapid, easy to budget for and to plan around.

Culture or operations changes can be therapy. It takes a lot of time, it feels like it's working, it's the best you can do, but the reality is you are fighting with the inevitable.

So to continue the strange metaphor, how do you have kids? How do you raise them? How do you give kids the best chance in life? If companies have kids it means creating new companies to take over.

You give them love, support and also the freedom to make mistakes. Ensure they learn as much as they can, especially when the stakes are not so high. Ensure that they have just enough money behind them in the background that they don't get lazy, or spoiled, or taken advantage of, but ensure money can always be found when truly needed to escape impossible situations, by buying time or life-changing opportunities.

## Step 3: Establish your specific approach to digital transformation

There are six broadly bucketed ways for companies to transform. What varies between them is:

1 Whether change is about building a new entity vs transforming what you have.
2 Which core competencies or domains change.
3 Whether the future entity is integrated into the 'parent' company.

### 1) THE 'HEDGE FUND'

A significant and increasing number of companies think that their future is best placed in the hands of others. Perhaps you think turning your company around yourself is just too hard, or that achieving growth by investing in other businesses, just as a private investor would with a share portfolio, is a sensible use of your company assets.

This model is based on the idea that the existing entity can't change that much, that fast, but that by investing in brilliant other companies which, vitally, you don't seek to change that much, you can manage your future by effectively spreading your bets on others. This effectively bolsters income and allows companies to place a variety of bets on the future, but also means you can't control or even learn significantly from these other companies.

A recent example comes from the huge Japanese mobile carrier, SoftBank. It's already a holding company with self-driving cars, energy-trading units and cloud services, and now it's leading a new fund, called the Vision Fund. It's raised $93 billion to do it, putting only $28 billion of its own money into it (Massoudi et al, 2017). It's often called corporate venturing, but some corporate venturing models allow for more interaction and learning between the parent companies and those they invest in.

The good thing about this model is that it allows for easier and simpler transactions and there is no complex integration required. The bad news is that there are few synergies from this transaction. There is no magic, it's just a linear acquisition no greater than the sum of its parts.

## 2) ADOPTION

This model is based on the idea that the existing entity can't change that much, but that by investing in existing brilliant other companies, which you seek to learn from and bring into your family, you can effectively bolster income and also inject key talent and assets.

The key difference between this model and the 'hedge fund' one is that you actively seek to take over the running of this entity and you also seek to integrate it into your company. Sometimes this may be about bringing in key staff, but it could also be about patents, assets, knowledge, market share or customer data.

When Walmart bought jet.com for $3.3 billion in 2016 (Lunden, 2016) it was not doing it for the same reason SoftBank may spread its bets on other entities. It was doing it to bring the skillsets, customer base and knowledge to help Walmart better attack e-commerce, hiring the industry talisman Marc Lore in the process.

These strategies typically suffer from complex integration challenges; often the startup that is required has been successful because of the culture and processes and talent in place. Trying to bring this into another unit is always very hard, but the benefits of this approach can be enormous and offer a magical combination of talent and scale.

### 3) INTERNAL VENTURING

This model is based on the idea that the existing entity can't change that much, but rather than buying new companies you try to develop new separate entities yourself. These are not huge existential bets on your future but a chance to develop a slightly wider product range, earn income in different ways, test and learn.

Midland Bank (now part of HSBC) was probably the first company ever to do 'a startup' when they set up First Direct. Created in 1989 from the need to find new growth, especially from profitable, reliable, affluent customers, First Direct started life as a blank sheet of paper with the word 'customer' in the middle. Inspired and intrigued by the idea of telephone banking, an entirely new company was created from nothing, but was based on the notion of reinventing everything in the banking model. They destroyed all conventions in the industry: the bank would be open 24 hours a day, would have no bank service charges, and would deliver helpful, unbureaucratic, unfussy, customer-oriented service.

The BMW i is a sub-brand of BMW founded in 2011 to manufacture plug-in electric vehicles. It's part sub-brand and part innovation lab for the main parent company. So far two

BMW i models have been made: the surprisingly practical i3 all-electric car and the i8 plug-in hybrid. BMW i series is now sold in 50 countries. While the unit itself has sold over 100,000 cars, it's unlikely to be close to being profitable by itself. Instead, the company is a feeder unit to the main company, developing technology to be used in other cars.

With these initiatives, the closer the new unit aligns with the core competency and depth of experience of the parent company, the more likely they are to cannibalize themselves. And they can also lead to complex internal cultural battles, where the culture of the new entity creates a sense of jealousy, and where the new units may feel hampered by the rules and requirements of the larger company.

### 4) PRUNING

Sometimes you have to accept you've got a lot going for you but change will be hard. And rather than seeking to invest in or build a new unit you decide to cut back on the services that you offer, and concentrate on those that are most appropriate for the future.

This model for change is rather like pruning a bush – get rid of the dead growth, cut back to something small. Get smaller to grow again faster or in a more profitable way, but from the same roots or base.

In the 1980s and 1990s, Jack Welch, the legendary CEO of GE, turned it into perhaps the biggest and most complex conglomerate on the planet. Yet under John Flannery it did the opposite, selling off elements like insurance and GE Capital, to focus its attention on what it believed it did best – making jet engines, power plants, and healthcare products like MRI scanners – and to stop making freight locomotives, microwaves, fridges, washers and TV shows via NBCUniversal.

In 2015 GE employed 333,000 people and had revenues of $94.4 billion; by 2019 it had reduced headcount to 205,000 people while revenues were slightly up to $95.2 billion (Mazareanu,

2021). This is less of a digital transformation strategy and more of a competence strategy but it makes the point. Dell shifted from being a B2C brand to a B2B seller of digital solutions and as mentioned before, when AstraZeneca doubled down on their core competencies, they started to outsource drug discovery to partners and other companies. Pruning seems to work, but to go back to go forward is sometimes a painful pill to swallow.

## 5) PIVOT

When you realize the current products or services aren't meeting the needs of the market, you can transform by pivoting. When companies do this they don't necessarily change size, they change direction. This may be a change forced by failure or one rooted in the new possibilities of technology or empowered by new trends or consumer behaviours.

In 2017, Nike introduced the 'consumer direct offence'. This included a shift to narrow the selection of retailers they would sell through while bolstering attempts to sell direct to consumers either via their own immersive stores or their digital channels, notably their suite of apps, including SNKRS, where they launched limited release products. These direct sales tended to have better margins, they gave Nike direct connections to customers and their data, and they allowed Nike more control of the brand. It's been a wildly successful shift from being a fashion brand to a retailer. In the company's 2021 fiscal year, ended May 31, direct sales rose to approximately 39 per cent of Nike brand sales, compared with 16 per cent 10 years earlier (Nike, 2021).

## 6) SELF-DISRUPTION

By far the riskiest, most aggressive, most potentially rewarding approach towards change is to self-disrupt. There are two clear elements that define self-disruption vs any other form of wholesale change.

Firstly, self-disruption has to involve a degree of cannibalism. The driving force behind self-disruption is to create a business that first wins market share and gains new customers, but ultimately should become so large and successful that it becomes the driving factor in the future of the company itself. This is wildly different to any other approach above and creates a widespread sense of alarm.

Secondly, self-disruption is rooted in the notion of acting fast, early and, most importantly, before you have to. If you buy a competitor that's rapidly eating your market share and ride on the back of it, this is merely a sensible acquisition strategy. It's investing, as most companies would, in protecting your position. What is key about self-disruption is that you act before many think you have to.

There are very few examples of self-disruption. Large legacy players are often too big, too reluctant to accept they are not right, too careful not to signal to the financial markets that they are somehow not already the best-placed company to survive. This way of changing is more likely to be used by smaller companies, ones with more to gain, yet often the smaller size of these entities makes them feel too vulnerable to pursue this course.

In two years of research, the best example of self-disruption I can find is Netflix.

Netflix's transition to streaming from DVD rental by mail was not nearly as smooth as many would like to remember it, but in hindsight it appears genius.

If Netflix had not disrupted itself it would be a very different company. It would rely on a massive physical distortion system, with very high costs. It would probably have lost out massively to YouTube and would have withered away.

### Step 4: Outline your broad company setup

Forget about the past and forget all assumptions. Forget about long-term leases signed, put at the back of your mind the effort put into acquiring company x, or the failed attempt to change four years ago, and ponder what your company would look like and feel like in order to best reach the vision you've set out.

Where would it be? How many people would it employ? What regular meetings would happen? What would you never seek to do yourself and instead outsource? What would your most valuable employees' skillsets be? What would you own? What roles would be consultants or freelance or part-time? What would you not do? Where would your offices be? What would you do in the office? What technology would form the basis for communication? Who would be on the board?

Operations comprises all elements of how a company works. It used to be the intersection of two things: the structure it has, and the process it follows. As needs evolved, it slowly included the idea of the people you employ and then more recently the technology you use, and perhaps even your data strategy.

Now all of these elements work in harmony. The people you employ have implications for your structure and your process. The data you access can inform process and structure. Technology can increasingly affect everything. So, knowing how to combine them all is hard. It rather reminds me of writing music. You can write the score, then fit lyrics around it, then find instruments to perform it. Or you could fix the instruments and then in a jamming session start to feel your way through the score. Or you could find a moment of inspiration on the train and suddenly start writing down lyrics and then find a score that fits them. Ideally, like musicians, we'd hold all ideas in our head simultaneously and constantly refine elements together in unison as a sort of iterative loop, but realistically we need to focus on and fix one element first, and that should be structure.

### Step 5: Design your structure

The structure is most simply described as the organizational chart. While in reality many companies have influence, information and commands outside a formal structure, we can't account for this and it's the chart that should be our focus.

One of the first questions to ask is how many people you need to employ and on what basis. Employment for millennia has been binary. You are either full-time and quasi-indentured, or you are unemployed. But the grey area is where it gets interesting. Especially in a modern working environment where presenteeism does not equate to value, access to the very best people on the planet often happens not through full-time employment but by other means. We now have an array of possibilities created by an environment of remote work. Part-time roles make more sense than ever: fractional roles, expert consultants to unleash value in quick doses, advisory positions to offer key wisdom and introductions, agencies to take on specific projects, and outsourcing, offshoring, partnerships and alliances to complete a toolkit of relatively unexplored parameters that have evolved recently.

WHAT YOU DON'T DO IS A KEY QUESTION

Companies of the future can be defined by what they don't do or own. Dropshipping creates the idea that I can sell my own label of cosmetics or style of jeans I've no idea how to make, and never touch or own, via a logistics firm in China, which I never visit, to a consumer anywhere on the planet, who I know better than most. By leveraging the power of both software and outsourcing, they become fulcrums to our minds that can move incredible things. GlaxoSmithKline don't have mechanics that service company cars. They focus on what they do best and outsource everything else.

It's not just that employing people is expensive, it's also that it's very inefficient. Large companies often seem to put more effort into maintaining themselves and what they do to progress, in the same way ultra-long-haul jets after a certain distance become oil tankers in the sky, burning their own fuel to carry their own fuel, with a few passengers on the side. Large teams are also slower to adapt and more likely to lose a sense of pride in some ways.

## WHAT IS THE SHAPE OF ROLES?

We should be aware of the value of generalists, especially when it comes to reducing headcount. We love the idea of the expert. We tend to assume that new technology needs a deep expertise. We think that everything that arrives is more complicated than we can imagine, and that we need to place our trust in people who understand everything about these technologies and these changes. Increasingly, the real success comes from building different bridges between different lines of thought – by connecting dots between two different disciplines. The very best minds on the planet are so driven and curious that they have a very wide range of skills and it's essential for them to add value by doing everything they can.

A good starting point for the future is to assume every role needs to be created from scratch. You need a brilliant reason to employ every single role. If it could be done as well anywhere else then it's not required. What is your core competency? What talent do you need some of the time? What are you uniquely placed to do? What roles can you not get the best people for? We should be mindful of the fact that the world's best minds in artificial intelligence may not want to work for a dog food company based in the middle of nowhere. It could be the case that brilliant graphic designers are not thrilled at the idea of only working on one client.

## WHAT STRUCTURE DO YOU USE?

This is not a book on organizational design. There are countless books about this vast area of expertise. I'm not here to explain it, to offer wisdom, but more to point out interesting questions.

Traditionally, organizational design is about optimization against two slightly contradictory ideas and goals: reliability vs adaptability. Reliability is a way to provide consistent products and services with minimal variation, to adhere to regulations and quality control requirements, a way to generate predictable returns for shareholders. Adaptability is the process by which companies can respond to changing needs; it's a way to try new things, to learn, to shift strategies and change tactics, to respond to changing demands over time or across the world.

Now that operational agility, quality of ideas, and retaining and nurturing brilliant, happy employees are perhaps more important than the requirements of the past, we face a different context. Technology has made it so much easier to keep track of each other and can offer two-way communication at scale, physical location has become less important, and there are a few new concepts to help resólve the reliability vs adaptability conundrum. Technology has raised the question of whether we need mechanistic organizations or organic ones. Mechanistic entities are like a machine that works systematically without any divergence from its standard path. The organic organizational structure is a flat structure where every activity is horizontal by nature. It is a complex system because there are no formal rules, regulations or guidance in place. Every employee is treated equally, hence interactions and communications dealings are placed at the same levels. The theory goes that organic organization structures emulate complex natural situations; they are suitable for unpredictable scenarios as the structure can adapt itself to any given situation. These are also often called 'poststructuralist', 'organic', 'post-bureaucratic' or 'decentralized' and offer, in theory, the best of all worlds.

What they have in common are the ideas that in the digital age, communication is easy, free and immediate, that companies should seek to distribute power in a decentralized fashion, and that staff members should feel a sense of belonging and autonomy. That quality of ideas and output should be maximized, not quantity or lack of variance. In the digital age, the company should work for people rather than the other way round.

Many modern thinkers think that instead of hierarchies with power coming from the top down, we should think of power as being at the centre of networks. Holacracy is the most popular form of this, a way for teams to be groups loosely connected but united by purpose. Consensual, democratic decision making, seeking everyone's opinion, is the norm – it all sounds rather pleasant but exhausting.

More lately, as the term decentralization becomes fashionable, we've seen even more radical ideas than holacracy, like decentralized autonomous organizations (DAO), which are entities with no central leadership. Decisions get made from the bottom up, guided and governed by a community organized around a specific set of rules.

Many of these drives to flatten companies are amazing as concepts but struggle in real life. Just as companies need reliability and agility, people need them too. Most people need to know who their boss is; most people need KPIs to guide them, they need known policies. We tend to not be that happy taking orders from people who are not paid more than us; inequality is a key dynamic in getting stuff done. Even though communication now scales more easily than ever and is cheaper and faster than ever, attention does not, our time does not, and it's relationships that tend to cement the best companies and departments. Sadly we are more like ants than wolves, and generally we like order, status and limits.

It's difficult to resolve many of the challenges in this area. There is no one-size-fits-all approach. Suitability depends on the kind of business you are in, your size, the talent you employ, and many other variables, but it's essential that you ask these questions and explore these options.

RETHINKING GOVERNANCE

Boards are there to represent the voice of shareholders, to focus on finance, to answer hard questions about legal issues, to digest risk, to discuss procurement and M&A, but never to consider their customers.

The board is the one safe place for wise, experienced folk to have the power and reputational capital to forge a compelling, ambitious, imaginative future vision. And yet the average age of directors in the FTSE 150 is over 60 and rising over the last decade (Hellier, 2017). I'm not suggesting we should idolize eight-year-olds who get TikTok, but to employ sensibly minded 30–50-year-olds seems to be a smart way to ensure an understanding of contemporary changes to the world, and the changing opportunities and threats ahead.

Boards appear designed to reduce risk, to preserve the status quo, to manage reliable but small growth and to ignore any potential. They seem often like a vessel to reward past service, more than drive energy into a complex future. They are home to accomplished people seeking to serve for years, not to challenge management orthodoxy, provoke brilliant debate or unleash the power of the new. Boards are recruited to find people more alike, from within a small pool of trusted people, and to embrace the comfort and ease of casual consensus.

## Step 6: Work around the power of new technology

Here's a question: how would you work today if you'd never known email? How would you work remotely if you didn't know that meetings existed?

Our emails look oddly like letters. Our Zoom calls look strangely like meetings. We've applied new technology to old processes, not rethought them. This needs to change.

In the olden days, operations was largely the intersection of structure and process. 'IT' was basically a support function. It was an administrative function, rather like stationery procurement, or finding office cleaners, or photocopier maintenance. They would be responsible for printer toner and for updating Windows 95; they didn't have the best offices and still don't.

Today IT should be one of the most vital departments of any company. It should be full of people excited about the future, investigating the latest software to do their expenses, enthusiastically testing new timesheet programs or better ways to manage invoices.

There is always a danger to adding technology on rather than rethinking processes. Bricks date back to 7,000 BC, which makes them one of the oldest known building materials, and while they are still rather useful, they do take a while to lay and bricklayers are in short supply around the world. Aware of this situation, New York-based Construction Robotics spent eight years of development to make SAM (Semi-Automated Mason), a robot bricklayer that can work 24 hours a day if necessary and can lay five times as many bricks as a human. It's a very impressive spectacle to watch this machine work, but in an era where construction could be changed for ever with advanced pre-fabricated modules, or 3D printing concrete, this solution seems like a rather strange and limited way to solve a problem.

One way to bring the power of new technology to the front is to ensure that profound new developments are showcased in front of the entire company.

Collaborative documents – cloud-based documentation infrastructure, even something as simple as Google Docs – have the ability to significantly affect the way we collaborate, but only when we rethink workflows.

A fairly typical regular process in many large sales-based organizations is to send out an Excel spreadsheet to each market. It could be a few, one to each headquarters, or it could be thousands, one to each unfortunate manager who then shares a copy around several people to complete, before gathering together several versions, copying and pasting data, and sending it all back to a global coordinator to spend hours cutting and pasting cells into one master sheet.

This document must then be sent to a senior analyst or region leader to assess, looking at the main trends and insights, and they may then make a few graphs and present the most interesting ones.

How much better would it be if data entry was done regularly and perhaps automatically in one central dashboard each day? For each individual it would take little work, and the analyst could view it any time they wished and at the press of the button all charts could be automatically generated.

Artificial intelligence and its several constituent elements like voice to text, image recognition or big data processing can have a particularly transformative effect but only when we use them at the very core of how a company operates, by rethinking workflows, policies and procedures. We think of automation as something that replaces people rather than augments them. The secret to using image recognition to analyse potential cancer victims' scans is not to ensure a doctor never has to see a scan, but to scan tens of thousands of images far better, and reduce down to a handful the ones that need to be passed to a doctor. Artificial intelligence cannot record a football match and make a brilliant four-minute-long highlight reel, as it has no taste or ability to craft a narrative, but it can listen to crowd noise, use spatial technology to know which camera to focus on, and then send 15 minutes of great footage out of 500 recorded minutes for a human to craft into those four minutes.

## Step 7: Rethink the processes

Process is how you work – the steps you take, the guidelines you work within and the workflows you typically follow. Process is seemingly an inevitable part of companies becoming larger. With very small entities it is quite easy to use guidelines, trust, regular observations and guidance as a way to ensure smoothness and repetition, but within a framework of ownership and pride. Conventional wisdom has always been that as you grow more rigid, process and thus policies and procedures are needed to govern everything from holiday allowances, expenses and recruitment but also the day-to-day activities undertaken.

The larger the company, the more likely these rules are to be tight, rigid and numerous. We all know they are for the greater good but often process, especially policies, can be rather limiting. If you buy a Mars Bar from a hotel minibar in Helsinki for $6 because you're working 18-hour days on an urgent pitch, your expenses will be declared void, but getting a taxi to a nearby restaurant and eating a $50 meal is no issue. You can invite 30 people to a pointless meeting with no agenda, start late and get little done, and few people seem to really mind because the $1,000–$10,000 'time cost' of the meeting isn't a 'hard' cost. The issue with most process is that it's there to stop chaos, not inspire brilliance – it's a safe way to manage yourself to averageness.

Start by evaluating your processes. It could well be that your radically transformed company has such a different structure, such different staff, such wildly new technology as a backbone that what you do now is irrelevant, but it's unlikely.

Since process is so readily absorbed as muscle memory and 'the way things are done', it's worth investigating and understanding all existing policies and procedures, from IT, budgeting, guidelines, workflows, best practice, frameworks or protocols to KPIs. Try to establish which of these are immediately essential and which are noticeably unhelpful.

Then, generate principles.

*Scaling Up Excellence* by Robert Sutton and Huggy Rao is a book that introduces the idea of the Catholic versus Buddhist approach to values and principles (Sutton and Rao, 2014). It's fascinating as it explains in a pithy style the way that entities best operate in the modern era.

For a long time, companies were like Catholic organizations: they wanted to create a strict doctrine of beliefs and practices, rituals and performances. A sense of dogged devout following, rituals and 'one way' of things being done, all with an underlying sense of guilt.

The future needs something else, as they call it, more like 'Buddhist' organizations. Those that are more open-ended, providing guiding principles but leaving details open to interpretation.

They tend to be able to travel across cultures much more effectively because it's the values that are being evangelized, not a rigid set of procedures.

Far more effective than the 3 Ps of process, policy and procedure is the one P of principles. It's a useful way to slowly strip away process.

There is no better company to follow for inspiration than Netflix in this regard. Netflix is not a perfect company and it's not for everyone, but it's useful to be aware of what they stand for.

Some interesting demonstrative principles from Netflix and beyond are:

- Know why you are doing something. Have a declared purpose. When people have a broader context of what their role is part of, it allows them to make better decisions themselves about what needs to be done, rather than relying on feedback. It also generates a greater sense of pride.
- Inspire people more than manage them; light a fire inside people, not underneath them. The role of leaders and managers is to guide this energy in the right direction.
- Trust is only earned when given. Trust people until they show you otherwise; similarly, assume good intentions until disproven.
- Give people freedom, power and responsibility. Many policies at Netflix, for example, are codified not by a staff manual and reams of paper but by the five words 'Act in Netflix's best interests'.
- Focus relentlessly on the future. Nostalgia is an early warning sign.
- Focus obsessively on what is best for the consumer. Perspective is invaluable; go to work ON the business rather than IN it.
- There is an assumption that people can't be relied upon to make sensible decisions. Encourage people to use their own judgement. It's a muscle that can be built by regular use.

- Impact is all that matters. Get stuck in. Roles are to be judged by the outcomes produced, not the process adhered to, or effort, or good intentions; your job is to make the greatest positive difference you can, which is ultimately always tied to actions.
- Finally, create key performance indicators that make sense.

In some ways, the only two things that matter in a role are where you get to and how you get there. How we describe and measure progress towards this is not a detail for those in talent departments to administer, but a massive strategic decision.

Companies over time often set KPIs that are focused not on the overall larger goals of a company but instead on the smaller and numerous strategies used to get to these goals. KPIs become smaller scale, more directly impacted, easier to measure, faster to change, and often the swell in their numbers can create such a rigid framework as to force people to behave in particular ways.

Let's say you're working as a CMO. Your role for 2022 may be to ensure a price increase can go through without affecting sales volume, and to slightly reposition your brand to demonstrate environmentally friendly credentials. Your progress could be measured by one KPI: profitability. This would assume that a price increase happened, didn't alter sales volume and the rebrand wasn't needed or happened well. Perhaps that's too vague and doesn't allow the board total visibility. Perhaps it could be:

1 Average selling price for 2022 is 5 per cent above 2021.
2 Sales volume 5 per cent above 2021.
3 Awareness of brand repositioning at Z per cent of current customers.
4 Key brand attribute of 'a sustainable company' up from X to Y per cent.

This gives four clear metrics to improve and you can develop your own strategy within them.

Yet all too often KPIs become stifling.

In order to push through increased pricing, we will ensure 10 of our 20 largest sellers agree to the price rise.

In order to ensure sales volume goes up, we will measure e-commerce and ensure it goes up 25 per cent, like our competitors. Let's ensure customer acquisition cost (CAC) is unchanged from last year and aim for a click-through rate of ads up Y per cent.

To measure brand changes, let's get a net promoter score of X, branded search volume should be Y, and share of voice up Z. Before you know where you are, you have no ability to make any decisions – you are held hostage by numbers.

## Seek to find ways to reinforce principles through policies

The importance of policy is massive in how it can signal intent. Find key but small-scale measures that can help articulate a new way of working.

One example is letting people update their own software on laptops. In a world where we ask people to make their own decisions and to take on enormous amounts of responsibility, it's embarrassing when you are unable to use your own choice of software.

Expenses can be another area. I've always toyed with the idea that all expenses should be placed on an openly accessible spreadsheet. People shouldn't be asked to defend them but they should be aware that they could be questioned. I've no idea how it would work out but it would be very interesting.

Another example is holiday policies. In many ways the policy of having unlimited vacation time has backfired, particularly in the United States, where it is used as a way for companies to avoid paying out holiday time accrued, but in many ways we can show clear examples of trust and freedom with responsibility.

A further key aspect is finding all the policies that can be removed without impact. Like a game of Jenga or Pick-up Sticks, slowly reduce bureaucracy until it is needed.

The more we look into policies like this, the more we must bring into question the idea of culture, which I explore in the next chapter.

## CHAPTER NINE

# A culture for transformation

Culture is an ecosystem, a cycle that maintains itself that is reinforced by policies, structures, power dynamics, physical spaces, rituals, processes, recruitment, training, precedents, celebrations, values and, above all else, bagels and maybe spreads too. It's an operating system that runs across anything and everything, and changing it involves considering the entire system.

## The fashion of corporate culture

I've spent a lot of time visiting client offices over the years and it's amazing how much you learn about companies from poking around their spaces. What is most amazing is the disconnect between what they say and what they have created. Between their past and their future intentions. The vast, forlorn, 1950s' out-of-town corporate campuses with peeling laminated posters asking staff to 'think like a startup'; the 'move fast and break things' sign next to a formal notice chiding those who missed the last health and safety training session; the neglected table tennis table in a faded, underused meeting room. Lots of people would love to ask for forgiveness and not for permission, but in a complex matrix organization, they're not sure who to ask.

Large companies are brilliant at being brilliant large companies. In the same way, oil tankers are great at carrying lots of oil, a long way, very cost-effectively. It's perhaps unfair to expect them to behave any other way. We don't berate container ships for not being great places for a boat party, nor do we think speed boats are poor for cargo capacity. The wonderful thing about the world is we get to choose, and rarely is there a better way, just a more appropriate one.

Large companies and their workers are a great match too. I'm not sure people who are doing a brilliant job in a vast blue chip multinational suburban headquarters, benefitting from great training, a generous benefits package, a pension, company car, clearly defined working hours and the chance of a placement in other markets, got in or stayed by mistake. I'm not sure they had dreams of working 15-hour days, with a low salary but equity for a bootstrapped startup in a trendy loft-style space in Berlin, but made a difficult, last-second choice to pick the one with a guaranteed parking space. We have to accept that people are very different, and by and large (and especially the most talented and driven people) we end up in the places we should have.

This doesn't mean companies shouldn't try to change, or to think that they don't need to, but it's to accept we need to be more thoughtful about understanding where these changes should be, and what they should change into and, most of all, *why* they should change.

After all, why should places want to act like startups when about 90 per cent of startups fail, 20 per cent within their first year? Only around 40 per cent of startups are profitable (Chernev, 2021). Why would companies seek to emulate this? Shouldn't festivals like SXSW be full of people saying, 'Act like an S&P 500 company returning consistent shareholder value by mitigating risk' or 'By all means move fast when it's vital to, but breaking things isn't the preferred way'? Shouldn't the corridors of fast-growing app companies have posters saying, 'Due diligence is the path to profit', or 'Think like Warren Buffett' (the longest-tenured CEO in the S&P 500).

The point here is not to be scornful, but we do need a slightly more mature and strategic approach to culture change, not one based on fashion. I have a firm belief that companies most often want the merchandising of change, to dress up like something else, but are rarely able to understand how hard culture change can be, why they need it, and what the changes they really need are.

In particular, companies seem to misunderstand the direction of causality in a great culture. A well-used pool table in the stock room likely first happened years ago because the staff got on well and found a way to bring in an old table one weekend. The pool table didn't make them like each other. In great companies, people like hanging out with each other. They may, by Thursday, start to feel the week is behind them, leave the office and head to the pub together to have some beers. Many companies seeing this have enacted Thirsty Thursdays, where beer and other drinks are passed around the office, and people chug drinks down alone at their desks. It all seems backwards.

## Culture and the third era of management

In an environment where command and control is the central way to operate, culture seems to matter less. When jobs are essentially about standardized processes, who needs diversity in the workforce? For years, organizations have focused maniacally on efficiency, reducing variation, consistency of production, and predictability. How does a happy workforce help here? Even as production moved more towards expertise and ways to add value to products in the production process or to include consumer understanding, the idea of culture being important seemed at best fluffy but, more realistically, indulgent.

In the new era, value comes from having not the most or the best staff, but the most engaged and inspired. It's no longer about quantity of time but quality of thought.

We now operate with a different managerial contract; no longer the command-and-control, top-down mindset prevalent in execution-type work, but more one based on inspiring people, persuading people. New theories of management have put far more emphasis on engagement of workers and motivation. We once felt as workers happy to have a job; now we may choose a place of work, not be chosen.

Your ability to influence is more important than your rank in the hierarchy. It's more important for leaders to have followers than subordinates. This is a whole new world where we seek different values and attributes.

## What is culture?

Everyone knows what culture is but it's very hard to define it.

The *Cambridge Dictionary* definition of culture is 'the way of life, especially the general customs and beliefs, of a particular group of people at a particular time'. Corporate culture is best explained as 'the beliefs and behaviours that determine how a company's employees and management interact and handle outside business transactions', which is still a nebulous way to think about a concept.

It's perhaps even harder to explain or measure when a culture is a good one – you can just feel it. It reminds me of the way that US Supreme Court Justice Potter Stewart once described pornography (to paraphrase): 'I don't know what it is, but I'll know it when I see it' (Stewart, 1964).

It seems few even understand what their own culture is; a Gartner Survey in 2018 found that only 10 per cent of HR leaders are confident that their organizations understand their culture (Gartner, 2018). It is often said that culture is what people do when no one is watching.

## Seven characteristics of 'company culture'

1  Culture tends to be tacit. While some companies may go to the trouble to describe what their culture is, in reality most definitions tend to be banal stereotypes, cliches and truisms that result from the collective gathering of sanitized statements and reduction by agreement. Most companies are not able to describe their culture – it's mainly something that is felt and seen. It is implied, not defined.

2  Culture shapes attitudes and behaviours in wide-ranging ways. In some ways culture is one of the most pervasive of all traits. It can and likely will reach every part of a company, have an impact on almost all decisions, and yet seem invisible. It exists across every department, across every level of seniority; it spans visible symbols, processes, language, behaviour, rituals, environments.

3  Culture is durable. Since cultural norms define what is discouraged, encouraged, rejected or tolerated and supported across a company, culture tends to ensure its own survival. It becomes self-reinforcing, especially via recruitment of people.

4  Culture evolves flexibly and autonomously. Culture is fluid. Like all social systems it tends to be tribal and chaotic. It may tend to follow some of the intention and spirit of top leadership but it can often be changed and modified via frontline employees, rumours, tradition and reward mechanisms.

5  Culture is invisible. Culture may manifest itself in furniture or as notices on community noticeboards but it is largely invisible. Culture is carried and created by the motivations of people, by collective unspoken assumptions, in mental models and mindsets, and approaches to almost everything.

6  Culture is shared. Rather like trust, culture can't exist in a vacuum or alone; it's about the interface between people and other things. Culture is only realized by the interactions between people. It isn't individual but group behaviours, values and assumptions.

7 Culture is a causal loop. It is self-sustaining and self-reinforcing. Behaviour will affect other behaviour, which may lead to policies or investments or partnerships which may then both reflect and create culture in the same vein.

There's a saying in the US military that if you see that something is low standard and you do nothing, you've just set a new standard. In some ways culture is defined by the worst behaviour you tolerate and the things you celebrate.

---

### WHY IS CULTURE THE LAST STEP?

Prevailing wisdom suggests that it's culture change that drives business transformation. That one can't alter structures or change or a company vision, products or ethos without first changing the culture. But it seems logical that it's far easier for talent and attitudes to fill the containers of new strategy, rethought and improved organizational structures and align to a brilliant vision than it is to hope a reinvigorated, energized, freshly recruited world-class workforce can maintain enthusiasm and commitment while the details of what they do, how they do it, and all the other vital elements of their work are resolved over a period of months or years.

So, while different from other models, the order outlined in this book is paramount. Fix the vision, which will act as a rallying cry, signal change to everyone, and give people a shared destination and purpose. Fix the structure and process and workflows in such a way that they reinforce the style of working with which you're most likely to succeed. Perhaps build out or buy trailblazing units that offer an exciting glimpse into what's possible and include brilliance that permeates the company. Then culture nicely fills out the spaces in between.

---

## The importance of culture

Culture has barely been appreciated for most of the industrial age. We still use terms like 'human resources' as a way to frame our most vital assets like a piece of flesh to extract value from. We talk of compensation as if somehow we are making amends for the fact that people are miserable. We have systematically dehumanized people, leading to management that seems to consider people like parts of a machine. The modern concept of the working week of five consecutive days, each eight hours long, doesn't come from the idea that eight hours is perfect for production or happiness but because it's a way to staff 24-hour production lines with only three identical shift rotations.

Yet in everything from legal firms to engineering offices, universities, architects' offices, consulting firms and advertising agencies, in the reported words of Narayana Murthy, founder of Infosys, 'Every night, your most valuable business assets walk out the door' (The Economic Times, 2013) – or at least they did in the age before remote working.

Having happy, inspired and hard-working people working for you is a key to success in the future, and perhaps your greatest competitive difference. As the value of great ideas becomes increasingly important, we should note that ideas are most forthcoming when the best people, working in a great environment, feel supported, valued and relaxed. New ideas make people feel vulnerable; support and psychological safety are essential.

By far the greatest advantage is that a strong company culture attracts better talent and helps retain that talent. A sense of belonging and shared values with the entity that employs you means you are way less likely to want to leave. People stay longer, which means less frequent new hires to deal with. Teams become stable, chemistry improves, there is a great chance of camaraderie. And of course recruitment, onboarding and training costs are lowered.

We've often assumed that the best talent is drawn to the highest salaries, prestige and imaginative benefits, but increasingly it appears that a sense of shared purpose, clear direction and a real sense that you can make a difference are now more important than ever. For years company culture has been a nice to have, but for these reasons, right now culture is vital.


## How do you change culture?

When we showcase companies with fantastic company cultures we often tend to use examples like Southwest Airlines, Zappos, HubSpot, Trader Joe's, Google, John Lewis, Nike or Apple. There are certain companies where great culture seems to emanate; anyone who has flown Delta and United, or Virgin Atlantic and British Airways, can somehow feel a positive spirit from Delta or Virgin, especially relative to their competitors.

But these are great examples of companies which have built fantastic company cultures and a motivated workforce – how many world-class examples of culture change are there?

Not many. To be honest, the scale of the problem may have been underestimated. As a reader, have you taken part in a culture change programme that has significantly changed the culture of any organization that you have ever worked in? Are there companies you interact with where you sense the culture has shifted? Your bank? Energy supplier? University? Retailer?

We may have misunderstood the brief; like many aspects of digital transformation, it is far, far easier to create than to change. Companies have been formed by repetition over decades or longer. They have been shaped like pebbles in a stream by years of reinforcement. Companies self-perpetuate. If we need radical change it would be more useful to think less of cultural transformation and more of cultural creation.

We need to go about the systematic process of adding to an existing environment the traits, personalities and behaviours that we wish to be emulated. It becomes a much better brief, not about destruction and wiping the past, but about adding the new. Creating culture is a much more empowering endeavour. What do we wish to amplify? Who do we want to bring in?

What should we add? What can we celebrate? This is a far better exercise. Above all else, and like all elements of innovation and business transformation, culture change is about growth.

## The five phases of culture creation

### Step 1: Audit of current culture

What are you dealing with? Companies do not end up with a culture and workforce purely by serendipity. A person can be offered and accept a job in a company that doesn't suit them, but people typically move on and end up in places where staff and culture are well matched. The comfy corporate campuses on the outskirts of pleasant satellite towns are not temporarily staffed by those who are about to launch their own company.

People usually end up working for (and staying in) companies that mirror the values and priorities they hold. Large companies offer prestige, stability, pensions, structured training programmes, employment benefits, world-class opportunities, and work brilliantly for those who are looking for that.

Best practice suggests robust interviews and tests against frameworks that measure values, mindsets, strengths, etc. We can put people through Myers-Briggs tests, or Belbin's Team Roles, or a 'Competing Values Framework'. In addition to these more scientific, objective, numbers-based approaches, we should undergo a richer, more nuanced, subjective approach. To simply use quizzes and tests and frameworks underestimates the degree to which culture is a rather magical thing. Having open, friendly, casual conversations can be far more revealing.

Ask people to be deeply honest about things like, Why did you join? What makes you stay? What is a good day? Who inspires you? What would you change? What is the worst thing that's happened? Who motivates you? What's the best thing you've done here?

It's risky, and only possible in an environment of strong trust and when framed as understanding, not judgement.

In his book *The Tipping Point*, Malcolm Gladwell describes three different types of people: Connectors, Mavens and Salesmen (Gladwell, 2000). I won't recount the book here, but it's well worth considering the people in your company that are more significant or vital than their documented role, or seniority, especially when it comes to culture.

A second theory is especially useful when it comes to knowing which staff are essential to keep and which are more likely candidates to move on, regardless of their expertise, outside relationships or reputation.

Michael O'Church, a machine learning engineer and active blogger in Chicago, casually introduced the idea of Adders, Subtractors, Multipliers and Dividers on the online platform Quora (O'Church, 2012). The theory is somewhat like this:

**Adders:** These are great team members, who deliver reliably and in a polished fashion. They know what needs to be done, how to do it, and do it well. They are individually capable of the work and they bring more benefits to the organization than their costs. They are never a burden.

**Subtractors:** These people generally have a negative impact, but not in a dramatic fashion. Their performance is lacklustre and not up to standard. They likely have the required skillset but their results are poor, they need surveillance to get the most out of them, never go beyond the minimum required, and end up as a distraction. It is possible to turn subtractors into adders through training or motivation, and they can often end up deeply loyal if this happens.

**Multipliers:** These are exceptional people, not just able to do what is required, but who go far beyond this. As individuals they are strong but they actively or passively motivate and help others perform. They are proactive, have leadership skills and collaborate well. They may question things but only to find better ways. They lift the team spirit through their work energy.

**Dividers:** Dividers are subtractors that not only cannot perform but also undermine and damage your team environment. They don't just not do the role but they create a harmful culture beyond their remit. They backtalk and form side conversations to bad-mouth someone or some decision. They are toxic to your team environment. The longer you have them, the more damage they will do to your team culture and morale.

## Step 2: Map out the desired culture for your company

Now that you have articulated your company vision and operations (Chapters 7 and 8), carefully map out your vision, your desired operating structure, the expertise and skills required and in which part of the organization. Appreciate that companies can't be cults, that values may differ, and that skillsets required align with personality traits. Not everyone can be the same. Be mindful that those working in roles in sales will likely be radically different in archetype than those in legal or IT. Be sure to find enough consistency for general alignment, but do not seek minimal variation.

### SKILLS ARE EASY, VALUES ARE HARD
So what are the desired traits you wish to see?

attitude to risk taking
sense of optimism
critical thinking ability
empathy
numeracy
ambition
honesty
loyalty

discernment
persistence and resilience
degree of urgency
willingness to have or give out power
sense of self-determinism
curiosity
agility
fun and humour

### DECIDE WHERE THESE CHARACTERISTICS ARE NEEDED

We are quick to praise rather clumsy mantras like 'creativity lies in everyone' or 'innovation is everyone's role', but is that true? There are a few issues. Firstly, why should we all seek to innovate?

The reality is that nobody is good at everything. In particular, the lively, discordant, playful brains that often explode with ideas or invention are not especially common, nor are they found routinely in all roles. Completer-finishers who thrive on paying attention to the smallest of details are simply not as proficient in innovation as big picture players with vision who never let reality get in the way and hate details – this is OK.

Innovation should not be in every role. I am sure the fine people who work at air traffic control should not be questioning how their job is done and experimenting with new ideas. Creativity can help a little in accounting but may not always work out well (hello Enron).

Similarly, as cultures become more aligned, they also have a tendency to become more cult-like. Like Darwinism, we need variance, exceptions, deviations, mistakes. Cults offer robotic sameness. The degree of alignment must ensure a company is not chaotic, but not so much as to streamline ourselves to averageness.

## Step 3: Create a plan to create this culture

Now, looking at the results of the audit and the culture and characteristics of staff required, have a sense of the degree of change you need. Does this instinctively feel like a question of iterative changes and small tweaks or is this about an utterly new outfit altogether? Is this about honing skills, polishing some elements, the surgical removal of some dividers, or have you ended up with a system ill-suited for the journey ahead? Either way, it's not sensible to seek to destroy your company's DNA, but instead to establish ways to build and amplify characteristics that will propel you to growth.

This is not failure. IF (and it's a big if) companies need to shift dramatically, we may have to accept that the skills and characteristics that got us here won't get us there. Based on these answers your approach will be very different in scale and ambition, but the following general principles still stand:

1 **Change should never be a mandate, it should always be a movement**
   It's about creating energy, persuasion and enticement, not about force, threats and demands.
2 **Change really occurs where there is a common understanding of a need to change and also of the end destination**
   Presenting and explaining a vision of where the organization should go is key. Communicate the desired vision, goals and culture, but also the process for change and establish (where possible) a commitment to action and to the future. When seeking to change Microsoft, CEO Satya Nadella introduced a new sense of mission with his employees: 'To empower every person and every organization on the planet to achieve more' (Microsoft, 2021).
3 **Establishing a leadership for change**
   Influence is interesting. There is a big difference between seniority and influence as we learn from Mavens and Connectors; those who make a difference are not ordained with power from a chart, but create it from bonds, respect, favours. So, pick key influencers. Messaging and change can come both from the top down but also the bottom up and from key people outwards. Culture is more freely spaced out.

4 **Invest in new talent**

Especially placing brilliant examples of the culture you wish to make in key influential roles. The benefit of new talent isn't just in what they bring, but in the messaging it sends across the company.

In many ways reality matters less than a plausible narrative. New hires do wonderful things for creating a sense of belief. They show dedication and confidence.

### Step 4: Create conditions to align with culture

The good news is that everything that you do helps create culture. The bad news is that everything you do helps create culture. Talk is cheap and actions speak. It's all too easy to announce intentions or initiatives but hard to create real change.

Again, since change comes from growth, create a multifaceted approach towards creating the culture you want. Conduct an assessment on every touchpoint that can be part of signalling who you want to be. Change the physical environment to reflect and allow for the acceptance of the new culture. If teamwork is the theme, rearrange the office to induce better teamwork; if safety is the theme, spend the money to make the physical conditions in the office, the factory or the service vehicles safe.

Policies are where verbiage turns into reality. They matter. What do your expense policies say? Your attitude to internships? Your hiring strategy? Everything you do says something.

The KPIs you use for people are another example. If you say that you are about embracing risk and testing and learning, or embracing failure, make the number of things you tried and the amount you learned from them a KPI.

Consider the benefits package; if you are about empowerment and letting people learn, how can the benefits you offer reinforce this?

Think about job descriptions. For so long we have defined requirements for people in terms of the role they do. We create narrow job descriptions based on fitting people into the most easily defined container. What if we considered roles as being more fluid, and we worked around extraordinary people we can find and let the value they can add be the starting point? How can we find extraordinary cogs and create the factory around them? Why not align incentives to match the culture?

## Step 5: Reinforcement and renewal – behaviours you celebrate

Transformation is not something that happens as a one-time impetus. It's an ongoing and everlasting and self-renewing process. We should establish mentorships with internal and external people and use this to offer a cost-effective way to support brilliant people.

Recruitment is the lifeblood of any company. It's how we grow and mature. Remarkable people are desirable on paper but when it comes to recruitment we seem to find people who are least likely to be a risk. We subconsciously seek to find people who are most like us, or people with credentials that make us feel less vulnerable in our selection. Let's be bolder and more interesting.

### RESULT-ORIENTED WORKING

Let's assume the CEO of a large company faces a hypothetical choice – either all of the staff he employs are able to accomplish everything set out for them every month without fail, but often finish work early, sneak in late, have sick days when not that sick, or he picks the other option where staff are perfectly punctual and hard-working, but routinely come short of what's expected of them. Which would they prefer?

At the end of the day, the only thing that really matters is what we are able to accomplish, both individually and collectively. Yet we don't tend to work with this focus on outputs, outcomes or results for a few reasons.

One, and it seems rather individualistic, is that there is a sense that if we were to work in this manner then we would only have a focus on things that are directly attributable to us. We may then end up ignoring things that are not measured as outputs, things like smiling in the office or helping people out when needed, or other less functional things. Similarly, most outputs actually demand working across large teams and often across departments, so how could we account for the idea that one person alone can't be responsible for getting stuff done?

But the main issue is that most roles are really about a mixture of rather soft metrics. Result-oriented working works very well in a sales environment, but not in most. Often the more significant and lofty long-term metrics that matter, that require lots of close working across teams, are turned into more short-term, more easily measurable, more precise proxies for these. So rather than measuring sales uplift due to brilliant marketing, we monitor how long it takes to answer calls, how many people click on websites, net promoter scores, and other rather daft numbers. Once these proxies become the metrics that matter we then change how we do our roles to optimize only against those narrow criteria.

The benefit of the ROWE (results-only work environment) is that we stop caring about how hard people work or how long people work and instead focus on what they accomplish. People who simplify their rules and do the things that matter well and are good with privatization intend to benefit under this system. As addressed in earlier chapters, a focus on fewer, bigger, more impact-related KPIs is the best approach, with the recognition that some aspects of outcomes depend on others, whereas outputs are normally more within our control.

## DECISIVENESS

In my experience one of the tragedies of the modern era has been that we now have so much data to rely on. As a result, we have lost faith in our ability to make decisions based on gut instinct.

Corporate roles have descended into risk avoidance and data as a way to pass on blame. Data culture has told us how we feel is wrong, it makes instinct feel undesirable, it creates risk aversion, we need consensus. This makes decisions slow to come about and reduces the chance of miraculous progress.

## MOMENTUM

There is a miracle to momentum. Making significant changes always seems overwhelming but it's like taking the first step in a marathon – we need to break down progress into smaller units and celebrate each success.

I always think about an aircraft on the runway. When it's stationary the engines need to suck air into the engines to drive it forward but because the plane is stationary the amount of air going into the engines is limited by the suction. The moment the aircraft starts to move, its forward momentum allows it to suck in more and more air easily. As it accelerates, the increased speed allows it to suck even more air even more effectively. Once at the speed it needs to take off, many of the forces holding it back are suddenly removed. The undercarriage slips into the airframe, and friction is immediately reduced significantly. The wings then pare back and the plane becomes what it's designed for.

The scale in all operations is to get to the point where the plane starts to move. A good way to do this is to think of all the barriers that we can remove, the impediments to momentum, and go through a process to streamline everything.

My hope is now not that you have a final, finished, typed-up presentation that outlines in enormous detail your future vision, the ideal operations, including your company structure, processes and procedures, a full brief for the technology that you are to build, a culture change strategy and a full acquisition plan. This is a book, not a multi-million-dollar consulting assignment we've undertaken over years. Nonetheless, I hope you leave these last three chapters in particular with a strong sense of the process that you should go through in order to develop a much more thoughtful process of change. I leave you now with the last chapter where we get to draw a line under the bigger theme in the book and set you on your way.

## CHAPTER TEN

# Rethinking your future

One of the most famous images of all time, The Blue Marble, is a photograph of planet Earth taken on 7 December, 1972 by the Apollo 17 crew from a distance of about 29,000 kilometres up. It's one of the most iconic and reproduced images of all time, and has been credited with starting the environmental movement. What few people realize is that the image we all see has been flipped. The original had the northern hemisphere at the bottom, which we know of course is 'wrong'.

The north and south poles are fixed by nature, not man. It's an axis we spin around, but when Earth is actually a sphere suspended in space, the idea that north should be at the top of maps is totally arbitrary, but universally understood to be 'right'.

What is fascinating is that maps are so significant both as practical ways to explore and understand the entire world around us but also as deeply symbolic in how we think of our place and context. Maps literally are our world view, our vantage point. It's rather apt that something shared by billions of people around the world, something so rigidly placed, is both totally explainable, utterly justifiable, indefatigable, but made up. It is a shared belief, not a fact.

So how much of the world, and indeed our worldview, is limited? What conventions can we challenge? How much of the world is fixed rather than movable? How many of these limiting parameters are reducing the scope of what we can accomplish and how many, like north and south on maps, are, while arbitrary, fairly irrelevant?

## Life is largely one-off paradigms

Anyone who has ever visited Los Angeles can immediately see and feel the problems of a city constructed around cars. Its urban sprawl in seemingly all directions, its endless traffic jams, its pollution. Upon landing in LAX, the crawling, chaotic traffic around the airport is a clear introduction to a city built around the excitement of the automobile in the late 1950s.

Fourteen per cent of LA County's land area is devoted to parking cars, 10 per cent is roadways for cars, and 40 per cent of the city is tarmac; it's a city designed in service of cars, more than people (Wattenhofer, 2015).

It's a celebration of freedom to travel. Distance becomes less important than time. It creates its own paradigm, and has designed 'feedback loops' which reinforce the current status quo, which just about works. You can wake up, get an elevator down to your car, drive to work, the gym, your doctor, the grocery store: a car-based life with abundant parking, air conditioning, making hands-free calls in traffic jams. Advances in technology like adaptive cruise control, lane assist or early self-driving car systems have made it less demanding to drive. Electric vehicles are now reducing pollution. With the advent of ride-share apps like Lyft or Uber, going on boozy bar crawls or avoiding crazy parking fees at LAX has never been easier.

At the same time, public transit is improving. Over the years, thanks to billions of dollars in investments, bus routes have increased in number and frequency and an extensive subway system with 93 stations and six lines has been constructed, with more in the pipeline. Other mobility solutions like Lime or Bird scooters have proliferated across the city. These incremental changes are slowly augmenting and improving the way people can move around.

So the question is, which system will win? As subway systems spread across the city, will scooters become vital last-mile options? Will delivery drones remove demand for goods delivered by road? Will roads and cars stop being the core element on which the city is based? Will there be a tipping point where we shift away en masse from cars, and where buses and scooters and bikes become so abundant they are preferable?

I think not. The entire city is oriented around cars. Using a scooter to get to a subway stop is horrendous and dangerous, cycling to workplaces with no showers is grim, and even walking to a grocery store across parking lots is undesirable. A high-speed railway may one day speed you from San Francisco to LA's Union Station, but you will still be miles away from your likely destination. It's likely Los Angeles will iterate within the paradigm of cars. It will build more freeways, it will invest in electric vehicles, self-driving cars will make things better, but the very fabric of the city is built for the car. The only way to change this would be to rebuild the entire city.

In order to change things, we need a new paradigm and to rebuild from scratch around the new design parameters of a new era. And we need to think of the digital world in the same way.

## A liminal moment

There is a palpable tension between profound possibilities opened up by technology and the way this challenges our preconceived ideas of how to live life. We have been programmed for scarcity, we work well with constraints. The past, rules of thumb, societal norms and our parents all provide us with a playbook for life.

Yet now technology offers us a whole new array of possibilities. When we work in jobs where our bodies don't wear out, the notion of retirement makes no sense. When hundreds of millions of people can vote for their favourite band on TV, why do we need governments to make decisions on our behalf? When we have access to the world's collective intelligence for free at any time, what do schools become? Why do we need to live in one place if our income is no longer tied to a place and time?

It sometimes seems that either we dare not question the core foundations of our lives or we simply can't imagine a future so wildly different. Physiologically our imagination and our memories are almost identical; when we remember the past, we use imagination to make sense of what we recall, but when we project into the future, we essentially use memory. Try to imagine a colour that doesn't exist, or design a future animal.

So we've augmented our lives. We use technology to pull through what we've seen before. We suffer the complexity and chaos of a mid-technology age.

Faced with technology altering many of the parameters of modern life, and a much wider domain of possibility, we seem rather paralyzed by choice, dispirited by stories of what we could be, and, well, a little lost. In some ways we feel a kind of new anarchy. A liminal point between paradigms, just waiting to build the future that we could have.

## What kind of future can we create now?

As we have seen, the first usage of steam power was to lift up water to power waterwheels, the first use of electricity was to replace steam engines, the first use of computing was to replace calculators, and the first use of the internet was to replace posted mail.

We should have learned by now that most technologies follow an S curve, where the degree to which a technology is diffused or deployed follows a series of steps.

Initially the technology is installed, and we see creative destruction, adaptation, social panic and confusion, a battle of old vs new ways of doing things, fragmentation and, increasingly, uncertainty and complexity.

Then we follow the creative construction period, a time where the technology is deployed, where people make new products and services around this – steam locomotives around steam power, refrigerators, radios and TVs around electricity, desktop publishing from computing, etc – and social benefits are unleashed.

Broadly speaking we have not yet got to the creative construction of much of the digital technology that surrounds us. We've had computing for over 50 years, but one could make an argument that we've yet to see even this taken to the very heart of what we do. More recently we've had billions of smart phones permeate the world, and we've had at first wired connectivity and now ultrafast mobile connectivity. We often celebrate some of the advances that we've made in the last few decades. Anyone can make a brilliant movie and post it to YouTube; we can set up stores that ship products we never touch, to any country in the world. But we've had very few profound inventions that have been created for this era. We've had very few genuinely significant changes to the way that we live our lives as a result of rethinking the world around the technology. This is a wildly exciting time to be building the future. But we have to be aware of one challenge.

## The problem of abundance

Part of the explanation is that we as human beings are not built for this age. Over millennia we have found our way as we grow up to make friends, form tribes, and make mistakes that we learn from. We are used to reputation existing as relationships within a confined radius of people, most of whom we've likely met many times. Communication for almost all of our existence has been one to one. The last few thousand years saw communication only as a tool for the wealthiest to reach a small number of people using seal skin or papyrus. The idea of mass communication, let alone mass communication from normal people, is utterly new.

We are not built for a period where social media can cripple the future of any young person who inevitably makes mistakes, where reputation can spread across the world in seconds, where intimacy can be asymmetric and people may know you far better than you know them.

As we have evolved slowly over centuries to crave fat and sugar, we've evolved for scarce information, and daily existential threats from other creatures, natural disasters, famine, and each other. We are programmed to respond to anything that moves in our peripheral vision and to find fear an essential way to keep alert and alive. We developed community as a way to come together, and religion as a way to cement bonds and give purpose to life and with it belief systems, symbols, objects, ritual and ceremony.

Centuries of evolution have created a body and mind optimized for an environment that has recently flipped. We are built for another era. In the words of Alan Gregg, 'The human race has had long experience and a fine tradition in surviving adversity, but we now face a task for which we have little experience, the task of surviving prosperity' (Gregg, 1964).

The problem of prosperity is a deeply provocative and uncomfortable idea. At a time when income inequality is so high, refugees swamp borders, the planet is warming and viruses are killing millions it seems abhorrent and ignorant to suggest we have enough, let alone that we may have too much.

## The key things to remember when building your future

### Picking the right time to change

I once saved up several weeks of hard-earned wages to buy a mini-disc recorder, so I know all too well the dangers of either jumping on the wrong technology or moving too quickly to embrace what is new. Most significantly, we do live in a period of time where significant developments in technology are coming our way. One could make an argument that robotics, automation and other elements of artificial intelligence could be so profound that we should seek to rethink and rebuild companies around them. I've always thought that artificial intelligence is the wrong way to think about it.

We should think of AI as augmenting intelligence. It is us, the humans, who have the intelligence. How can we use computing to undertake the jobs that don't need our brains and bodies and free up our time to add the most value, which will always come from us doing the most human things, using our empathy, ability to connect, imagination and creative problem solving? Remember, the deeper you apply technology, the harder it is, but the more powerful it is as a lever for change. So how can we apply new developments at the core?

### Change comes from growth

As I've spent months toiling on this updated version of this book, it hits me that it's been far harder and far more time consuming to write this book as an update to an older one than it would have been to start from scratch and create an entirely different book. Which, given that a central premise of the first version of this book was that it's much easier to construct than it is to change, gave me a constant sense of irony.

Companies often want to cut their way to growth, an approach that both signifies a desire to change and also has the benefit of improving the P&L in the short term. Yet we all know that in order to change, we have to invest in ourselves.

We may need to accept that companies are like people and they are destined only to live for a certain period of time. Evolution relies far more on mutations in our DNA and the process of birth than it does on us adapting while alive.

## We don't so much change culture as add a new one to replace the old

We should less pivot into a new strategy but more build a new entity around a new, better idea. We should focus far more on the dynamics of growth and addition than of reorientation, reprogramming and the pain of change. Which is great because building is way more fun than destroying.

## The 2 Ps of innovation – problems or possibilities

There are two ways to innovate. By far the easiest, most common and most likely to succeed is to work around a clearly defined problem. This typically already provides the genesis of the idea, leaps of faith are not hard, and ideas of this nature are quite easy to get buy-in on.

Tinder was a way to meet people with less effort, Instacart or Deliveroo help lazy people get food without doing anything, Juul delivers us nicotine with potentially fewer health issues and less smell. Kayak makes it easier to get a flight.

A harder way to innovate, which can lead to more outrageous levels of success, is to work around the possibilities that technology offers, but only if they are profound enough.

DJI drones and Tesla exist because of improvements in batteries. Facebook can dominate media because technology allows anyone to create content for free. While the latter can be far more profitable, it only works if the new possibilities of a technology are clear and it involves little behaviour change. Virtual reality and Blockchain both seem rather problematic in that they don't yet solve key problems, and the promises of what they could make possible are perhaps less than enthusiasts suggest.

## A more predictable future

Few things attract more scorn at dinner parties than saying you are a futurist, so I don't. The reality is that the future is not as poetically unknowable as we often like to think. Yes the resolution of predictions isn't huge – we can't predict winners of horse races or world cups – but getting a higher-altitude picture isn't hard.

Tech doesn't change who we are, it changes some of the mechanics of how we do things. Social status was once just conveyed by items we held, but now it can be projected by photos we have of experiences we access, or just images of the things we once held.

At our core we need to stay alive and procreate. In order for us to do this we need people to like us, to respect us, to want to have sex with us, as well as food and, in some climates, a roof. An app like Tinder is not representative of a wholesale change in human nature. It's just a new way to do what we've done before. Facebook isn't a new behaviour, it's gossip and small talk on a global network.

Generally speaking, the stuff that really matters changes the slowest and is easiest to predict; fads are immediate and live and die in seemingly arbitrary ways; fashion is a little slower but still rapid and deeply hard to predict; commerce beyond this – how we spend our time, where we go and what we buy – is slower, but increasingly easy to predict. Things like infrastructure and regulation are painfully slow to change, and elements like human nature or societal etiquette are slower still.

Unless you are in the business of selling barbecues before random hot spring days, or jumping on search data to ship this year's Christmas toys before others, most business happens at layers that are slower to change, and more predictable. E-commerce is not a trend that has come from nowhere, working from home has been predicted for years, and our consumption of more media and in digital ways is not a shock. Even the Covid-19 pandemic, when we look back on it in the future, will have done little to change core elements of what we do.

But more than anything else, most companies are based on what stays the same and most of life remains close to how it's always been. We can project into the future changes, but if we do so with similarities the picture is clear.

## Challenge assumptions

Disruption is really the art of questioning the right assumptions. Trump's first presidential race put the person with perhaps the least knowledge of politics in the most powerful role on the planet. Did he do this despite his lack of knowledge or because of it? I'm not advocating idiocy, but I'm saying in many ways expertise has become dangerous.

The more we know, the more we tend to become entrenched in a viewpoint. We seek to make sense of the world, and to understand it in a way we find comforting, more than we seek to challenge it.

In the 1960s, Warren Buffett joked of taking advice from old investors: 'They know too many things that are no longer true' (Buffett, 1969). In the early 2000s the top car makers in the world were paying the best experts in the world to tell them that what Tesla was doing was impossible.

*Disruption is really the art of questioning the right assumptions.*

Clearly, we cannot wake up every day and question everything. It is sensible to assume that gravity exists, to think that your mobile phone is telling you the correct time, and that you should wear clothes outside. But in order to live a more efficient life we may have got into the habit of never questioning ANY of the parameters in our lives.

Life is a constant battle between the expressions 'we tried that before and it didn't work' and 'this time it's different'. The skill is in knowing what assumptions to question and how and when. A good way to do this is to imagine how other people would approach your situation.

## Be committed, not agile

'Move fast and break things', 'Test and learn', 'Dynamic optimization', 'Fail fast' – we've all embraced the thinking of the modern age and this 'always on' and agile approach.

Clearly moving fast is good, and clearly bureaucracy is bad, but sometimes we default to fast over good. As software starts to dominate the world, the culture of shipping fast, shipping often and fix it later is replacing the idea of doing things properly first time.

iOS 6 was a huge upgrade to many people's iPhones – it was the one where the icons moved to being flatter looking. Since the launch of iOS in 2012 we've had 46 major updates to it, and at the time of writing we're at iOS15, but I can't remember anything big ever changing. Each and every year software is updated more often, every single version becomes far larger in size, and typically nobody can remember any benefits. What would have happened if in the last nine years and 46 software updates Apple had instead tried to make one amazing new operating system for the phone?

Often corporate strategy for large firms seems to be missing. There isn't a bold vision, progress is an algorithm, we A-B test ourselves to the future. This isn't inherently bad, but it reduces the chance of bold progress.

In companies over the years I've seen servers that are littered with the remains of moderately ambitious change 'initiatives', a well-intentioned plan to move to shape shifting, a new culture of constant learning; I've seen histories of bold ideas, without the energy, funding or focus needed to ever carry them out. I've seen reorganizations become a near-annual event.

What if we need the opposite of agile? We need sudden leaps to a new way, then stability while we adopt it, embrace it, and to maintain that form until it becomes out of date. We need to leap and then stick. We need continual 4- or 6- or 10-year plans. We create brand new entities on the latest thinking and software and all the time have people working on planning what the next leap will be.

## Simplify and focus

When I was working with Nokia in the early 2000s, each and every year we launched more phones. Fashion phones, music phones, imaging phones – the very same year that the iPhone launched we had introduced 72 new handsets. Clearly focusing on one device that would change the world would have been a better strategy.

It sometimes appears that companies are determined to measure progress by busyness. And the word 'yes' is the most powerful career accelerant. We seem to embrace the concept of more, more quickly than better.

It seems that the environment of working from home in particular has reduced the degree to which people feel comfortable having the slightly harder conversations that involve the word 'no'.

Increasingly, your company should be defined more by what it doesn't do than what it does. And what it does best should be the driver of all strategy. Establish what is uniquely special about your brand, talent, intellectual property, etc and focus rigidly on ways to use this brilliance to carve out a space in the marketplace and consumers' lives that you can dominate.

## Be proactive

The benefits of changing before you have to are huge. Unfortunately, by far the greatest motivators of change are urgency and necessity, which are also the worst possible environments in which to do it.

We may like to think that we rise to challenges but few things limit problem-solving abilities, imagination or creativity like anxiety, stress or urgency. Just imagine being told to come up with a great idea at gunpoint.

Companies that have struggled to adapt to the world are rather like the proverbial frog that's boiled to death. If it was immersed in a pot of boiling water it would jump out straight away, but if the temperature slowly rises, it doesn't see the danger in the same way and by the time it needs to leap free, it's nice and relaxed, incapable of mustering the energy.

Not only does changing early bring about more time to change, but it brings about a different mindset. With proactive change you are able to control the process; it's no longer dictated by others and their new products or consumers and their changed habits, but on a timeline and in a manner that you dictate.

Proactive change feels exciting. It becomes an opportunity that you are exploring, not a challenge you are reluctantly gathering around. A key skill is finding the right amount of importance and immediacy to bring about a key shift, in a way that also maintains calmness and optimism.

## A focus on empathy, not technology

A cruel irony of the modern world appears to be the negative correlation between many people's interest in technology and their interest in people and how they live their lives. It's equally ironic that most of the people who are in sectors where their roles depend on understanding how normal people live also tend to live some of the most abnormal lives.

The greatest opportunities in the world today come from understanding the needs of normal people. We've been tricked into thinking that all technology starts as a toy for rich people before moving down, and use this to ignore the realities of billions of people's lives. We always look at target markets in aspirational ways; we envision the lavish lives of Peloton owners, or the needs of affluent millennials in apartments in Shoreditch or Williamsburg, over farmers in Kenya, or middle-aged accountants in small towns.

We need to get much better at understanding the meaning of technology, not just what it does. We need to consider core human characteristics: do people want to stick AR glasses on their heads? Is part of the social acceptance of mobile phones that we know at least when people are distracted?

We need to think much less about the technology itself and more about the implications when technologies mature, combine, influence regulations, change societal expectations, change fashion or behaviours. We need to think more about the interactions between technology and other changes in the world. How does the connected age and a growing movement to preserve our planet change the broader environment that we live in? How does it affect attitudes towards consumption, or towards travel or relationships?

## Diversity

Diversity has become a huge conversation in the 2020s, but it often seems to be based in the idea of fairness. That recruiting from my diverse background is a morally 'good' thing to do. It often seems to be done from a fairly defensive and almost cynical place, the focus typically only on some forms of diversity, especially those that you can see and measure easily. This approach is bafflingly stupid.

The clear reality is that pulling together people from a range of backgrounds is quite simply the best way to work. Almost every single process in the world benefits from having a variety of inputs. Evolution itself is rooted in variance.

And diversity covers an array of differences. Our focus recently has mainly been on internal diversity characteristics, ie situations that a person is born into like race, sexual orientation, gender, nationality or disability.

Yet the wonderful array of differences that we can use to power progression lies beyond this. We need far more acceptance of the notion of class in many industries and the brilliant people this mindset stops us drawing from. We need to approach age with more enlightenment; we readily worship the energy of youth, but we need to have a much smarter approach towards the incredible benefit of wisdom, maturity and context from those who are far older. Diversity is everywhere. People learn in different ways, have different political opinions, come from wildly different backgrounds of income or geography, have different approaches to risk, different skills and knowledge.

We have an incredible width of neurodiversity, we have extroverts and introverts, we vary in ideologies, morals, values and ethics.

Given this politically charged and challenging context, we've become rather lazy. For too long we've recruited people who are good enough and the most alike. Subconsciously it seems we'd all rather be in a meeting with people who like the same sports as us, who also think Person X is amazing, and Y is an idiot. We like talking to people who may have read the same books as us, and may know the same people from university. We are lazy. At some point we decided that the people that we work with should all be quasi-friends, that interactions should be smooth, and that, well, we don't need to learn much.

To work with people who are like you is to remove all the potential to learn from almost every single event or moment. Collaboration has rightly become a celebrated part of the modern business process. But all too often what people think of as successful collaboration is not a process that gets to a better output, but a process that seems fair, is polite, doesn't involve too much debate or emotion, and is comfortable for all.

The wonderful thing about how different we all are is that it allows us to unleash the energy of discourse. Collaboration isn't neatness – it's passion, it's stress testing, it's new ideas thrown into the mix, it's challengers, it's robust, well-intentioned probing.

We need a much more sophisticated approach to diversity, and that comes from knowing why we do it and what outcomes we want. It's my passion that we should do it because it's far harder, far more interesting, and a far more likely way to succeed. But we need to want it.

## Ambition and risk

At this precise moment in time the job market has for years been one of the best we've ever known. There has probably never been a better time to get fired. In many ways, it's one of the least likely times to get fired. And yet the pervasive sense of anxiety in the way the people go about their roles has never felt more real, intense and extensive.

I am never really able to understand this. What's the worst thing that can happen? In many ways the better things have got, the more sensitive we have become to slight discomfort. What's the greatest risk you've taken personally in the last three years? What's the greatest risk you've taken professionally? Was this a career- or life-endangering move?

In particular, decision making seems slowed by the modern age; we now seek data, not gut feelings. Data is rarely about making better decisions, it's about taking the blame. Data is the perfect thing to blame because it won't get offended and it won't argue back, and because every decision rooted in data looks objective, not emotional.

In many ways the greatest danger to most people living in the modern age is that of living an unremarkable life. We need to rethink our goals less around threats and more around maximizing possibilities.

Who were you before the world started getting in the way and dictated who you are? Why are we so scared to be wrong? Scared to feel alive? Why are we scared to accomplish what we are capable of? Who or what is holding us back?

## Urgency

There's a popular Chinese proverb that says, 'The best time to plant a tree was 20 years ago. The second-best time is now.' It's quite pithy but a little annoying.

I don't think we realize the power of this moment. We are often waiting for something – permission, a business case, a new technology. The inescapable truth of the business world is that we seem to be using the excuse of faster change as a reason to do nothing.

The past is a great way to learn, to contextualize things, to get perspective; the future is an essential focus for any company, and imagination about what will happen and what you can do is essential. But the only time we can ever take action is now. Your future is being built by the quality of your present moment. You are co-creating reality RIGHT NOW! You can start singing your favourite song, you could down a tequila, you could this very second go for a walk, or phone a lost friend. This isn't the sort of book to tell you to do that, but it's an undervalued idea that we are all in control of almost everything we decide to do in the next second and the next second. And like compound interest, the mathematical magic that is compounding returns works even better for people who make sustainable changes to their lives.

Is life ever not this moment? Reality is now. Nothing is more powerful than now, and recognizing the significance of it. It's the only moment we have to act – other than memories or imagination, it's all we have. All we have is now.

# References

## Preface

Fowles, J (1974) On chronocentrism, *Futures*, **6** (1), February, pp 65–68

Graeber, D (2015) *The Utopia of Rules: On technology, stupidity, and the secret joys of bureaucracy*, Melville House, Brooklyn

## Chapter 1

Ang, C (2021) Which countries gained (and lost) the most millionaires in 2020? *Visual Capitalist*, 3 February, https://www.visualcapitalist.com/changes-to-the-worlds-millionaires-2020/ (archived at https://perma.cc/3MD2-KV39)

Brumley, J (2021) Netflix is losing market share, but this is the actual risk to shareholders, *The Motley Fool*, 15 April, https://www.fool.com/investing/2021/04/15/netflix-is-losing-market-share-but-thats-not-the-a/ (archived at https://perma.cc/ZC7L-CM33)

Del Rey, J (2020) The US government is breaking up Big Razor before it gets to Big Tech, *Vox*, 11 February, https://www.vox.com/recode/2020/2/3/21120169/harrys-ftc-acquisition-edgewell-schick-gillette-dollar-shave-club (archived at https://perma.cc/YP5D-QEGT)

Kim, T (2020) Airbnb and DoorDash broke the IPO market: Here's a fix, *The Economic Times*, 15 December, https://economictimes.indiatimes.com//markets/ipos/fpos/airbnb-and-doordash-broke-the-ipo-market-heres-a-fix/articleshow/79737491.cms?utm_source=contentofinterest&utm_medium=text&utm_campaign=cppst (archived at https://perma.cc/SB3E-CA43)

Lerner, K (2016) House Republicans shut off cameras after Democrats start sit-in for gun control, *Think Progress*, 22 June, https://archive.thinkprogress.org/house-republicans-shut-off-cameras-after-democrats-start-sit-in-for-gun-control-5538c7345965/ (archived at https://perma.cc/JA9U-7KMZ)

Pressman, A (2020) Snowflake's shares soar 112% after IPO, *Fortune*, 16 September, https://fortune.com/2020/09/16/snowflake-shares-soar-after-ipo/ (archived at https://perma.cc/JA7T-XT8X)

Proceed Innovative (2021) Google dominates worldwide search engine market share [blog] *Proceed Innovative*, 10 February, https://www.proceedinnovative.com/blog/google-dominates-search-engine-market/ (archived at https://perma.cc/AN7C-96UK)

Reuters (2008) Man auctions off his life, sale price disappoints, https://www.reuters.com/article/us-auction-odd-idUSSYD21931720080630 (archived at https://perma.cc/FM9Y-F9JM)

S&P Global (2020) Era of buybacks under threat as rising debt meets politics, ESG, *S&P Global*, 25 August, https://www.spglobal.com/marketintelligence/en/news-insights/latest-news-headlines/era-of-buybacks-under-threat-as-rising-debt-meets-politics-esg-59641671 (archived at https://perma.cc/D39P-EUCF)

Scinto, R (2020) Tesla celebrates start of leasing cars in Connecticut, *Patch*, 12 February, https://patch.com/connecticut/milford/tesla-celebrates-start-leasing-cars-connecticut (archived at https://perma.cc/EWS7-NME8)

Sheeler, M (2021) Everything that's (still) wrong with Amazon, *34th Street*, 16 March, https://www.34st.com/article/2021/03/amazon-criticisms-avoid-online-shopping-amazon-jeff-bezos (archived at https://perma.cc/QC4F-MNXN)

Yakowicz, K (2019) 14 months, 120 cities, $2 billion: There's never been a company like Bird. Is the world ready?, *Inc*, https://www.inc.com/magazine/201902/will-yakowicz/bird-electric-scooter-travis-vanderzanden-2018-company-of-the-year.html (archived at https://perma.cc/Y3XS-UWM5)

## Chapter 2

Levie, A (2014) [tweet] https://twitter.com/levie/status/488509773361324032 (archived at https://perma.cc/L9YL-9395)

Phys.org (2006) Hybrid cars – pros and cons, 19 January, https://phys.org/news/2006-01-hybrid-cars-pros-cons.html (archived at https://perma.cc/T49S-E4AC)

## Chapter 3

Adner, R (2012) *The Wide Lens: A new strategy for innovation*, Portfolio Penguin, New York City

Clark, A (2007) Wear a watch? What for? *CBS News*, 16 February, https://www.cbsnews.com/news/wear-a-watch-what-for/ (archived at https://perma.cc/S63N-Z3AV)

Haire, M (2009) A brief history of the Walkman, *Time*, 1 July, http://content.time.com/time/nation/article/0,8599,1907884,00.html (archived at https://perma.cc/ZT88-SSW5)

Kaufman, G (1998) MPMAN threatens conventional record business, *MTV*, 4 May, http://www.mtv.com/news/150202/mpman-threatens-conventional-record-business/ (archived at https://perma.cc/8NKF-DWPQ)

Kuhn, T (1962) *The Structure of Scientific Revolutions*, University of Chicago Press, Chicago

Ramey, J (2021) Tesla made more money selling credits and bitcoin than cars, *AutoWeek*, 27 April, https://www.autoweek.com/news/green-cars/a36266393/tesla-made-more-money-selling-credits-and-bitcoin-than-cars/ (archived at https://perma.cc/9T8D-92XL)

Rodic, D (2017) CEO of 'bed in a box' start-up Casper on going from zero to a $500 million+ company in 4 years, *CNBC*, 14 June, https://www.cnbc.com/2017/06/14/casper-ceo-philip-krim-on-becoming-a-500-million-company.html (archived at https://perma.cc/C4V2-V5BA)

Twain, M (1889) *A Connecticut Yankee in King Arthur's Court*, Charles L Webster and Co, New York City

Van Buskirk, E (2005) Bragging rights to the world's first MP3 player, *CNet*, 25 January, https://www.cnet.com/news/bragging-rights-to-the-worlds-first-mp3-player/ (archived at https://perma.cc/5T92-XRFZ)

## Chapter 4

CNBC (2018) Nestle to pay $7.15 billion to Starbucks to jump-start coffee business, *CNBC*, 7 May, https://www.cnbc.com/2018/05/07/nestle-to-pay-7-point-15-billion-to-starbucks-in-coffee-tie-up.html (archived at https://perma.cc/69XY-W8U6)

Drucker, P (1959) *The Landmarks of Tomorrow*, Harper, New York

Hamel, G and Breen, B (2007) *The Future of Management*, Harvard Business Review Press, Boston

Kelleher, K (2017) Andreessen was right: Hardware is hard, *Pando*, 22 February, https://web.archive.org/web/20170704024026/https://pando.com/2017/02/22/andreessen-was-right-hardware-hard/ (archived at https://perma.cc/X4VV-HPCK)

Porter, M (1996) What is strategy? *Harvard Business Review*, November–December, **74** (6), pp 61–78

Prahalad, C K and Hamel, G (1990) The core competence of the corporation, *Harvard Business Review*, May–June

Starbuck, W (2005) 'Bureaucracy' becomes a four-letter word, *Harvard Business Review*, October

Taylor, F (1911) *Principles of Scientific Management*, Harper & Brothers, New York City

## Chapter 5

Cox, K (2021) Software bugs reportedly keep Arizona inmates jailed past release dates, *ARS Technica*, 22 February, https://arstechnica.com/tech-policy/2021/02/software-bugs-reportedly-keep-arizona-inmates-jailed-past-release-dates/ (archived at https://perma.cc/9KA6-7WFY)

Debré, E (2021) How a software error made Spain's child COVID-19 mortality rate skyrocket, *Slate*, 25 March, https://slate.com/technology/2021/03/excel-error-spain-child-covid-death-rate.html (archived at https://perma.cc/8XRA-Z88F)

Loosemore, T (2016) Digital: Applying the culture, practices, processes & technologies of the Internet-era to respond to people's raised expectations, *Twitter*, 10 May, https://twitter.com/tomskitomski/status/729974444794494976?lang=en (archived at https://perma.cc/Q2CJ-KJHJ)

McKay, D (2020) What is COBOL, and why do so many institutions rely on it? *How-To Geek*, 15 April, https://www.howtogeek.com/667596/what-is-cobol-and-why-do-so-many-institutions-rely-on-it/ (archived at https://perma.cc/Y4GZ-VUNV)

Millman, D (1984) *Way of the Peaceful Warrior: A book that changes lives*, H J Kramer, Tiburon

Smith, A (2019) NHS relies on over 1m computers running Windows 7, *PCMag*, 31 July, https://uk.pcmag.com/old-news/121891/nhs-relies-on-over-1m-computers-running-windows-7 (archived at https://perma.cc/5D8L-EAJ6)

Stack, L (2019) Update complete: US nuclear weapons no longer need floppy disks, *The New York Times*, 24 October, https://www.nytimes.com/2019/10/24/us/nuclear-weapons-floppy-disks.html (archived at https://perma.cc/ZK27-NEU4)

Whitwam, R (2015) 48,000 PCs at Fukushima plant operator TEPCO still run Windows XP, *Extreme Tech*, 23 April, https://www.extremetech.com/computing/204056-48000-pcs-at-fukushima-plant-operator-tepco-still-run-windows-xp (archived at https://perma.cc/58EF-4TLS)

## Chapter 6

Kalinin, K (2021) How to create a neobank from scratch in 2021, *TopFlight*, 21 July, https://topflightapps.com/ideas/how-to-build-a-neobank/ (archived at https://perma.cc/49P8-Y9UB)

Mlitz, K (2021) Spending on digital transformation technologies and services worldwide from 2017 to 2024 (in trillion US dollars), *Statista*, 23 August, https://www.statista.com/statistics/870924/worldwide-digital-transformation-market-size/ (archived at https://perma.cc/CVV5-KLB4)

Nordström, K and Ridderstråle, J (2001) Funky business: Talent makes capital dance, *Financial Times*, London

Sull, D (1999) Why good companies go bad, *Harvard Business Review*, July–August

## Chapter 7

Amazon (2020) Our mission, https://www.aboutamazon.co.uk/uk-investment/our-mission (archived at https://perma.cc/9GAM-28BE)

Christensen, C M, Cook, S and Hall, T (2005) Marketing malpractice: The cause and the cure, *Harvard Business Review*, 83 (12), December

Christensen, C M, Hall, T, Dillon, K and Duncan, D S (2016) Know your customers' 'jobs to be done', *Harvard Business Review*, September, https://hbr.org/2016/09/know-your-customers-jobs-to-be-done (archived at https://perma.cc/W45J-M473)

Gray, A and Kruppa, M (2020) Lululemon buys fitness tech start-up Mirror for $500m, *Financial Times*, https://www.ft.com/content/d301fead-2d88-4d26-934c-c54b54b16d13 (archived at https://perma.cc/6KUM-CQ39)

IKEA (2021) Vision, Culture and Values, https://ikea.jobs.cz/en/vision-culture-and-values/ (archived at https://perma.cc/96PA-3SK9)

Samsung (2018) Samsung Electronics Sustainability Report 2018, https://images.samsung.com/is/content/samsung/assets/global/our-values/resource/Sustainability_Report_2018v3.pdf (archived at https://perma.cc/R8VV-RLQM)

Schopenhauer, A and Saunders, T (1893) *Studies in Pessimism: A series of essays*, S Sonnenschein, London

Southwest Airlines (2020) Our Vision, https://careers.southwestair.com/culturetemplate (archived at https://perma.cc/77QQ-5N5C)

Walgreens (2021) Vision, https://news.walgreens.com/press-center/frequently-asked-questions/vision.htm (archived at https://perma.cc/Z5X4-DC2M)

WeWork (2021) The beginning of a new story, 8 January, https://www.wework.com/newsroom/wecompany (archived at https://perma.cc/MML3-CBHR)

## Chapter 8

Drucker, P (1954) *The Practice of Management*, Harper & Row Publishers, New York City

Hackl, E (2017) *VIS-À-VIS Medien.Kunst/Bildung*, edited by Stean Sonvilla-Weiss, De Gruyter, Berlin

Hellier, D (2017) UK board members are growing older as European firms look to youth, *The Independent*, 19 December, https://www.independent.co.uk/news/business/news/uk-business-board-members-older-eu-firms-youth-ftse-stock-index-aged-over-60-a8117731.html (archived at https://perma.cc/S8KA-AH4Q)

Lunden, I (2016) Confirmed: Walmart buys Jet.com for $3B in cash to fight Amazon, *Tech Crunch*, 8 August, https://techcrunch.com/2016/08/08/confirmed-walmart-buys-jet-com-for-3b-in-cash/ (archived at https://perma.cc/2AAZ-VYB6)

Massoudi, A, Inagaki, K and Hook, L (2017) SoftBank's Son uses rare structure for $93bn tech fund, *Financial Times*, 12 June, https://www.ft.com/content/b6fe313a-4add-11e7-a3f4-c742b9791d43 (archived at https://perma.cc/DV2C-ZEJ4)

Mazareanu, E (2021) Total number of employees at General Electric from 2006 to 2020, *Statista*, 16 February, https://www.statista.com/statistics/220718/number-of-employees-at-general-electric/ (archived at https://perma.cc/ZHR4-4HZN)

Nike (2021) Investor news details: Nike, inc. reports fiscal 2022 first quarter results, https://investors.nike.com/investors/news-events-and-reports/investor-news/investor-news-details/2021/NIKE-Inc.-Reports-Fiscal-2022-First-Quarter-Results/default.aspx (archived at https://perma.cc/B7B6-RSWL)

Sutton, R and Rao, H (2014) *Scaling Up Excellence: Getting to more without settling for less*, Currency, New York City

## Chapter 9

Chernev, B (2021) What percentage of startups fail? [67+ Stats for 2020], *Review 42*, 16 November, https://review42.com/resources/what-percentage-of-startups-fail/ (archived at https://perma.cc/A3DP-489G)

Gartner (2018) The CHRO's Guide to Culture, 12 February, https://www.gartner.com/smarterwithgartner/the-chros-guide-to-culture (archived at https://perma.cc/B7B6-RSWL)

Gladwell, M (2000) *The Tipping Point: How little things can make a big difference*, Little, Brown and Company, New York City

Microsoft (2021) About – our mission, https://www.microsoft.com/en-gb/about/https://www.microsoft.com/en-gb/about/ (archived at https://perma.cc/C3EQ-HDHF)

O'Church, M (2012) How do you fire an employee that just isn't good enough? *Quora*, 8 September, https://www.quora.com/How-do-you-fire-an-employee-that-just-isnt-good-enough (archived at https://perma.cc/D4R8-TSUE)

Stewart, P (1964) US Supreme Court, Jacobellis v. Ohio, 378 US 184

The Economic Times (2013) Has Narayana Murthy's return at Infosys worked for the IT major?, *The Economic Times*, 8 September, https://economictimes.indiatimes.com/tech/ites/has-narayana-murthys-return-at-infosys-worked-for-the-it-major/articleshow/27845971.cms?from=mdr (archived at https://perma.cc/D4R8-TSUE)

## Chapter 10

Buffett, W (1969) Partnership letter, May 1969, https://www.gurufocus.com/news/6620/warren-buffett-partnership-letter-in-may-1969 (archived at https://perma.cc/Q5PP-KUKZ)

Gregg, A (1964) Acceptance speech special award, 84th annual meeting Lasker Awards Ceremony, November 12–16

Wattenhofer, J (2015) 14 percent of Los Angeles County land is dedicated to parking, *Curbed Los Angeles*, 30 November, https://la.curbed.com/2015/11/30/9895842/how-much-parking-los-angeles (archived at https://perma.cc/K4V7-YHX3)

# Index

Page numbers in *italic* indicate figures or tables

# HOW TO FUTURE

## LEADING AND SENSE-MAKING IN AN AGE OF HYPERCHANGE

SCOTT SMITH
WITH MADELINE ASHBY

Kogan Page
INSPIRE

# THE INFINITE LEADER

## BALANCING THE DEMANDS OF MODERN BUSINESS LEADERSHIP

CHRIS LEWIS
PIPPA MALMGREN

Kogan Page
INSPIRE

# BEYOND

## HOW TECHNOLOGY IS LEADING
## A PURPOSE-DRIVEN BUSINESS
## REVOLUTION

# GOOD

THEODORA LAU
BRADLEY LEIMER

Kogan Page
INSPIRE

# NATHALIE NAHAI

BUSINESS UNUSUAL

VALUES, UNCERTAINTY and the PSYCHOLOGY of BRAND RESILIENCE

Kogan Page
INSPIRE

CPSIA information can be obtained
at www.ICGtesting.com
Printed in the USA
JSHW052249280422
25413JS00008B/65